THE LEA[RNING LOVE]

MW01291123

HANDBOOK

A SERIES OF BOOKS FOR LEARNING THE ART OF LOVING AND INTIMACY

BOOK II

HEALING SHAME AND SHOCK

Dr. Krishnananda Trobe, M.D., and Amana Trobe

Founders and Directors

The Learning Love Institute

Sedona, Arizona USA

TABLE OF CONTENTS

INTRODUCTION:

T his is the second in The Learning Love Handbook series. Each book has been written to correspond to a guided meditation CD with the same title sold separately.

Our motivation for writing this handbook and particularly this edition is to present a method for working with troubling and complex psychological issues in as concise and simple a way as possible.

This edition is about *self-love and regaining our positivity*—how we lost it, how we may continue to lose it, and how we can rediscover it.

Three mind states block our ability to love ourselves and to feel positive about our lives.

These three states are fear, insecurity, and self-judgment.

They can be so deeply ingrained into our way of thinking, being, feeling, and acting that they can literally run our lives.

We may feel too afraid and discouraged to take the steps we need to create the lives we would like.

We may not even know what steps would help.

Our fears and insecurities may be continuing to cause us to experience failure and rejection in such a repetitive and painful way that we feel helpless and in despair.

Or we may feel that life is unfair, unkind, unsupportive, and unloving.

We may be chronically critical of ourselves or of others.

We may be afraid to look into a mirror for fear of seeing ourselves as too old, fat, collapsed, frightened, negative, false, insensitive, weak, dumb, or lazy.

We might experience moments of intense fear that we cannot explain or contain.

We may find ourselves crippled with fear and insecurity.

Overcoming such powerful mind states as shame, self-doubt, collapse, depression, fear, and shock is no small thing.

We, the authors of this book, have struggled with these states in our own lives, and at times, it even felt as if we couldn't see any light at the end of the tunnel.

But from our personal experiences, we know it is possible to work through these mind states and come out the other side.

It is not simple, or quick, or easy.

There is no simple tool that corrects our difficulties.

The journey back to self-love and positivity is a journey that takes time, commitment, and perseverance.

But it is a very rewarding journey that not only brings relief from the torture of shame and insecurity and the paralyzing experience of shock and fear, but that also brings tremendous depth and sensitivity.

We cannot pretend or promise that by giving you some simple steps your sun will shine forever.

We all have and will probably continue to have dark moments of shame and fear.

But we can reach a point when they no longer run our lives, and we can learn to be more gentle and loving with ourselves when these dark moments come.

In this handbook and the CD that accompanies it, we will provide you with some guidance to overcome these negative mind states.

Part 1 deals with insecurity and self-judgment that is called **shame.**

When we are taken over by shame, we are deeply convinced that we are basically defective, deficient, wrong, unattractive, unlovable, or bad.

Shame is a powerful hypnosis that can easily and frequently take over our minds, inner experiences of ourselves, and our behavior.

It is a false but highly compelling negative mind state.

We can transform it in six essential and crucial steps that we will be describing in this handbook.

The first step is *to understand* what shame is, what causes it, what triggers it today, how it affects our senses of self, what it feels like, how we think, and finally how we behave when we are in shame.

The second step is *to enter into shame with awareness.* From the vantage point of adulthood, we now have the strength, awareness, and resources to experience it both as it occurs today in our lives and also as we felt it as children.

The third step is to cultivate regular and consistent ways *to move our life energy with song, dance, sports, or training.*

The fourth step is *to take small but consistent risks, and strengthen our resources and sense of ourselves.*

The fifth step is *to transform our negative self-judgments with compassion and understanding.*

And the final step is *to persevere* in spite of discouragement, frustration, or setbacks.

Part 2 of this handbook deals with **fear** and its silent, frozen, and often hidden state, **shock.**

This is a second mind state that often blocks our ability to love ourselves and to enjoy life.

Fear can hold us back from living our lives as we would like, from making necessary changes, from expressing ourselves, from opening our hearts, or even from relating at all.

Fear can contract our lifestyles and our bodies, cause sickness, profound mistrust, or rejection, and give us the experience that life is passing us by.

It can cause us to live in continual compulsive reaction for fear of being hurt, abused, ignored, or taken advantage of.

It can cause us to live in continual compensation by puffing ourselves up, becoming fanatic about a belief system, pushing to be perfect or the best, or its opposite by collapsing and giving up.

In its active form, fear can cause us troubling panic attacks, restlessness, hyperactivity, hypervigilance, inability to focus or concentrate, or insomnia.

In its frozen form, fear can cause us to become confused, forgetful, tired, dissociated, or overwhelmed, to override our boundaries, or to misuse our bodies.

Our common approach toward fear and shock is often to judge, ignore, deny, and avoid them.

But this approach only causes greater suffering and self-hatred.

In this section, we will be describing a way to transform our fear and shock, to discover their hidden treasures, and to integrate and incorporate these two experiences into our lives and senses of self so that they produce depth, sensitivity, and compassion.

PART 1

UNDERSTANDING AND HEALING SHAME AND INSECURITY

CHAPTER 1:

WHAT IS SHAME?

The word *shame* can be confusing.

What we mean by *shame* is an experience of ourselves where we feel:

- That we are in the wrong or inadequate.

- That we don't measure up.

- That we are defective, wrong, bad, useless, incapable, and not as good as we should be.

- That we are continually judging ourselves or comparing ourselves to others.

Shame is an experience of not being in contact with our gifts and our purpose in life. It is a deep feeling of disconnection from existence, of not knowing who we are and what we have to contribute in this universe. It is like a huge identity crisis.

Because of not feeling ourselves from the inside and not recognizing or trusting our gifts, we have turned all our energy outside and become very attuned to how other people want us to be.

So we no longer live according to our wisdom but try to fit into what other people want us to be.

We have given up our authenticity and become compulsive joiners.

Once we have given up being true to ourselves, we are naturally very sensitive to any kind of criticism.

All this is shame.

We can experience shame in three ways.

The *first* is how shame *feels as a body experience.*

It normally comes with a lack of energy and motivation, a feeling of tiredness, contraction in the chest, tightness in the belly, depression, inability to start anything, hopelessness, and being sick or feeling pains in the body.

The *second* way we may experience shame is in *negative judgments or shame thoughts*—judgments of ourselves, others, or life in general.

We may not be aware what our mind is saying, but if we explore the phenomenon of shame more deeply, the judgments become clearer.

And from the space of shame we can easily feel guilty, feel that we have done something wrong, that someone is going to punish us because we were bad, or that people won't respect us because we did or said something stupid.

Some examples of typical judgments are: "No one loves me, I don't deserve love, I will never be good enough, I am a bad person, I have to be the best, I am a loser, the world is a hostile place, I can't compete with other people, I can't trust anyone, I don't have anything to give, I feel overwhelmed, there is no point doing that."

Finally, the *third* way you can experience shame is with what we call *"shame behavior."*

Common shame behavior can include: compromising, being unable to set limits, being attracted to people who humiliate us or are not available, doing things that are self-destructive, using drugs, developing eating disorders of all kinds, having weight problems, isolating ourselves, compulsively wanting attention, being dishonest, not initiating new things, bragging or exaggerating our accomplishments, or giving up on things that we start after a little discouragement or small setbacks.

Shame can be acute or chronic.

Acute shame is provoked by criticism, judgments, rejection, failure, or moving out of our comfort zone by expressing ourselves in a way that is new, going to a new environment, or studying something new.

When we experience one of these shame triggers, it is very likely that we will have what we call "a shame attack."

A shame attack feels as though all of a sudden, we have lost the wind in our sails.

We have suddenly lost our confidence, hopefulness, enthusiasm, joy, excitement, energy, and love of life.

Everything seems dark and desperate and we are not sure if it will ever come back.

Chronic shame is different.

With chronic shame, we may not be able to identify a trigger.

We might not even be sure why we feel this low.

Perhaps we have felt like this for so long, we don't know what it is like not to be in shame.

When we have chronic shame, we constantly have low energy, depression, and lack of motivation, which may result in our complaining or easily giving up.

Actually, in most cases, the insecurity, lack of confidence, fears, and negative beliefs about ourselves have been with us as long as we can remember.

Perhaps we did not know what was behind these feelings or that it had a name, but we knew that we were feeling inadequate and without confidence.

We thought it was how we are, always were, and always will be.

Most of us have some level of chronic shame, but some of us have found better ways to compensate for it so as not to feel it.

We may be able to cover our shame with compensations for a long time. (This is a topic we will discuss in the next chapter.)

But then we may have an accident, get sick, lose someone we loved dearly, or experience a financial setback, and all of a sudden, all the shame we have avoided feeling all of our lives comes up.

Whether we have recently gotten in touch with our shame or whether we have felt it for a long time, sooner or later we will have to confront it and heal it.

We came into this life with a natural sense of joy, curiosity, open-heartedness, trust, and innocence.

But we lost it somewhere along the way.

Somewhere and somehow we got distracted from our true being.

In this little book, we will take you on a journey to heal your shame and recover the natural self-love that you lost.

Exercise

Take a moment to consider this space called "shame."

- Has this been a factor in your life?

- Is this still something that you experience regularly?

- How have you tried to avoid it?

- What provokes it in your life today?

CHAPTER 2:

WHY AND HOW WE RUN AWAY FROM OUR SHAME

The first stage of our journey is uncovering the ways we might be hiding our insecurities, fears, and feelings of inferiority from others and from ourselves.

Who wants to feel insecure or who wants to admit that he or she is insecure?

Would you? Who would want to feel insecure?

What is your opinion about your own insecurity and fears or about other people who are insecure or afraid?

Perhaps you judge them?

Perhaps you were raised to be successful and judged when you failed?

Or perhaps you were shamed for being afraid and told that you should stop being so emotional?

If we have been raised in such a way that success is given the highest value and failure is looked down upon, it is natural to believe that our worth depends on how well we do.

Our lives become more and more focused on winning and feeling ashamed of our failures.

Our lives become focused on getting approval from others and hiding our insecurities and fears.

As a result, we may find all kinds of ways to hide our shame.

We may build a lifestyle around pretending and avoiding situations that could bring up shame.

We invite you to ask yourself:

- "What do you not want someone to know about you?"

- "What do you do that makes you feel worthwhile in the eyes of others?"

- "What do you do that makes you feel unworthwhile in the eyes of others?"

Different Ways of Hiding Shame

Peter is a thirty-six-year-old software engineer who has a high-level job in a successful computer company. He has a soft-spoken, gentle manner and seems sensitive but timid and introverted. As he talks about himself and his life, he says that he has been successful in school and now in his work life, but admits that his relationships with women have always been difficult even as a teenager. He doesn't think that he is "man" enough, he has a hard time approaching a woman he is attracted to, and all his relationships have ended in painful rejection. When he is with a woman, he is so afraid that he will make a bad impression that he often cannot think of what to say. In lovemaking, he is convinced that he is a terrible lover because he is so tense that he generally comes too fast. Now he feels hopeless and discouraged, and he has avoided making contact with women altogether. He prefers to spend his days devoted to his work and his evenings watching television.

Matthew is a successful forty-two-year-old lawyer who is a partner in one of the largest law firms in the city where he lives. He drives a fast Italian sports car, wears elegant clothes, and spends his holidays skiing or going to expensive beach resorts. He is charming, self-assured, and articulate. He says that he feels quite confident with women and thinks of himself as a good lover, but he is afraid of losing his freedom. So when things get "too complicated," he leaves. As one might expect, he chooses glamorous women to be with, but complains that he has still not met the "right" woman—"they all want to spend my money and they are all so superficial." Also, sexually, he finds that he gets quickly bored with the same partner.

Stephan is thirty-eight years old, runs a business with his older brother, is married, and has three young children. For years, he and his wife have been in conflict because when Stephan is disturbed, he shouts at her. He gets upset when the house is not as clean or as tidy as he would like, when she doesn't take care of practical things at home, or when the children are too loud or wild. He also yells at his employees at work when they are not doing things the way he expects. His wife is threatening to divorce him because of this behavior, so lately, he has been able to get somewhat more control over his anger, but he sees that there is something much deeper inside that he has to deal with.

Susan is a thirty-seven-year-old pediatrician who is fulfilled at work and financially comfortable. Her problem is with men. Her pattern is to attract men who enjoy her sexually but who are unwilling or unable to commit to a more ongoing relationship. She is furious with her latest boyfriend because after they had dated for months, he decided that he preferred only to be friends because "things were getting too complicated." Even though Susan is convinced that she does not want to continue only on this basis, and that it is not good for her, they continue to see each other, and she leaves him feeling frustrated, cheated, and abused. This is the third relationship in a row in which she has felt rejected.

When her father died three years ago, thirty-five-year-old Alexandra retreated from life. She had been extremely close to her father, who treated her as his special one above her two older sisters. In fact, she had even felt that he preferred her to her mother, and in some ways, even though he had never invaded her sexually, she had felt more like a lover than a daughter. To please her father and earn his respect, she had excelled in school and in sports, was captain of her volleyball team in high school, and then later became a lawyer just like him. She has not had a relationship with a man that lasted longer than several months because she felt that nobody could compare to her father. Now she is clinically depressed, has stopped work, is drinking heavily, and generally feels hopeless about life.

All five of these people are hiding their shame in one way or another.

Peter is hiding by isolating, Matthew is hiding by creating a false image of himself, Stephen is hiding his shame behind his anger and his obsession with perfection, Susan is hiding behind a pattern of chasing men who are not available, and Alexandra is hiding her shame by becoming depressed and drinking alcohol.

Peter has deep shame in his relationships with women, but, rather than face and work through his shame, he has chosen to eliminate this troublesome aspect of his life. He no longer puts himself in situations in which he feels attracted to women or has to ask them out and receive another rejection. He prefers to avoid them altogether.

Matthew is not even aware of having shame. He has created a lifestyle that is an excellent compensation for feeling vulnerable. He has used his gifts of intelligence, social ease, and confidence as a man to succeed in work and in his sex life. By doing what he is good at and by keeping his relationships superficial, he does not have to run the risk of feeling insecure or being rejected.

When Stephen explodes with rage, he is unaware that underneath the anger are a great deal of insecurity, feelings of unworthiness, and a deep fear of not being good enough as a man. He places so much importance on his work, on the work of his employees, on the order of his house, and on the insistence that everything is taken care of according to his standards because his sense of self rests on things being the way he wants and feels they should be.

Instead of acknowledging how insecure she feels as a woman, Susan gets angry at and blames the men who reject her. She has not realized that the men are reflecting her own rejection of herself. She is *"shame shopping"*—entering into relationships with unhealed shame. People who "shame shop" send out the message "I deserve to be rejected." Susan is projecting the energy of someone who does not love herself, but rather than feel this shame, she escapes into blame and anger.

Alexandra hides her shame behind mystifying her father. As her father's special child, she created a fantasy of herself as "the special one" To hold on to this fantasy, she never allows herself to really open up or become vulnerable to another man because it might threaten the fantasy. She believes that she needs a strong man, but no man is ever good enough. Her relationships with men have been a poor substitute for her father's love and adoration, and now that he is gone, she feels like she has lost the only true love of her life.

The behaviors that we use to hide our shame we call *"shame compensations."*

Let's look at some others.

- We may hide our shame by playing *the victim,* getting chronically sick, feeling sorry for ourselves, blaming, or complaining that life or other people are unjustly treating us, not appreciating us, or ignoring us because we don't want to feel our own haunting sense of inadequacy.

- We hide our shame behind *addictions* such as gambling, abusing alcohol, or using other substances so that we don't have to feel the pain inside.

- We hide our shame by *giving up, not finishing, or sabotaging* what we begin, or by avoiding taking risks or expressing ourselves because we don't want to face the possibility of failure.

- We can hide our shame by *rejecting people before they reject us or by avoiding deep intimate relationships* so we don't have to face the shame of rejection.

- We hide our shame by adopting *rigid belief systems* and arguing for them.

- As in the case of Stephen, we often hide our shame with *anger, bouts of negativity, pouting, throwing tantrums, and slamming doors.* We get angry when other people or the world doesn't live up to our very high standards. Those standards of perfection become the very foundation of shame.

- And finally, another common way of avoiding feeling shame is by *wielding power and control* over others in any way we can—through money, position, giving or withholding sex, seduction, taking care and taking responsibility of others, or spiritual authority.

All of these compensations become habitual ways of behaving that may have been ingrained in us since childhood. Often we use our natural gifts, skills, and strengths as our preferred way to avoid feeling shame.

We have no way of knowing that we are avoiding something deeper inside until we begin to develop an inner sense that we are running away from something.

How can you feel that you are living in compensation?

- The state of living in compensation has a definite energetic quality that you can feel in your body—a certain *tension and contraction,* maybe resulting in shallow breaths.

- It has a *sense of falseness,* a lack of authenticity, a feeling that you are pushing, running, and hiding.

- You may notice that *people have a hard time coming close to you* or opening up to you.

- You feel a *constant sense of malaise* because you are not connected to yourself, to others, or to what is happening around you.

- You are *missing a deeper meaning in life.*

Exercise:

Take a moment to reflect on what you have been doing or are still doing to hide your shame.

- Write down these behaviors.

- Take a moment to feel how you feel inside when you are behaving this way.

- Can you sense what you are running from?

CHAPTER 3:

THE COMPENSATED-SELF

Before we can take the journey of healing shame, we have to reach a point in our life when we are ready and willing to go look behind our compensations.

So, let's take a closer look at what compensation is and how it covers our shame.

Imagine that you are living in a building with three floors.

On the top floor is what we call *"the compensated-self"*; on the middle floor, *"the shamed-self"*; and on the bottom floor, *"the real-self."*

Let's look at some examples of people who are living in the compensated-self layer.

Roberto works as a financial consultant in a large investment firm. His days are long and stressful, and in the evenings, he often goes to bars with his colleagues and drinks heavily. He says that alcohol allows him to fit in and to feel that he is the leader of the group because when he drinks, he feels confident, relaxed, and articulate. He doesn't like it when he feels insecure, afraid, and shy, particularly among his coworkers, and he also judges these aspects of himself with other people he meets. He says the reason he has been successful at work and is respected by his bosses is that he has hidden his fear and pushed through it. Furthermore, he cannot imagine that any woman would appreciate him if he showed his insecurities.

Roberto's situation is not uncommon. He is fortunate, unlike many people who live in the compensated level, in that he at least recognizes that he has deep fears and insecurities. But because he judges them and attributes his social and work success to his compensations, he is not yet motivated to accept his shamed-self. He does not see the value of shame.

The compensated-self hides the shame behind all kinds of behaviors, masks, addictions, distractions, self-images, and roles. In the compensated-self, we push ourselves to live up to our own expectations and to the expectations we grew up with. We will use our natural gifts such as physical beauty, intelligence, athletic ability, high energy, or creativity to strengthen our ego and create a sense of self that gives us love, respect, power, and wealth.

Andy is a wealthy businessman whose motivations in life are the pursuits of money, power, and sexual experiences. He prides himself in being generous to those less fortunate than he is by donating to charities, but he has no idea that his life is really empty of meaning and love. His ex-wife admits that she enjoyed the luxury of their lifestyle and his generosity while they were together, but she felt that she could never come close to him. His sexuality was exploitive and often abusive, and she sensed that he was constantly trying to prove his sexual prowess to her and himself while they were making love. He treated others more as objects than people and could never admit to his own weaknesses or insecurities. Finally, when she discovered that this relationship was a self-destructive, shame-based relationship for her, she found the strength to leave him.

When we live in the compensated-self, it is hard for other people to come close to us because what they experience is a wall of denial and pretense. They experience someone who is not authentic because he or she is not in touch with his or her sensitivity, limitations, or fears.

In the compensated-self, we are desperately afraid (often unconsciously) to expose the shame because we may be convinced that people will judge and reject us if we do.

However, living in the compensated-self is not in tune with our being.

- We may feel *lack of real connection with anyone.*

- We may *burn out* from pushing ourselves so hard.

- We may *get ill* from abusing alcohol or substances or from living with such a frantic pace.

- We may *destroy a marriage* or relationship by not allowing ourselves to be vulnerable.

- We may have a serious *accident* because we are moving so fast.

- We may have a *financial meltdown* because we have taken unconsidered risks.

- We may become *depressed* because there is no meaning in our lives.

- We may alienate or *become distant from our children.*

Do you think that you have reached a point in your life when your compensations have become too costly for the quality of your life?

Roberto, the financial consultant we talked about earlier, has begun to seriously work with himself and his shame. He has attended several seminars and is committed to weekly individual therapy with one of the authors of this book (Krish). He recognized that his compensations and alcohol abuse are affecting his life, entered a twelve-step program, and is now sober. He also recognized that the way he was living was dishonest and disconnected from his feelings and his soul. He wants intimacy in his life, and he wants to be an honest person. He now knows that he is covering his shame, and he feels ready to explore it. He is still afraid that if he admits his shame to himself and shows how frightened and insecure he feels, especially with women, he will be judged and rejected. But because he is now ready to expose himself, his relationships are changing. He still judges his fears and shame, but by admitting to having them and being guided to feel them with Krish, he is noticing that he is not feeling judged or humiliated but is beginning to feel like a deeper and more human person. Six months prior to this writing, he began a new relationship with a woman whom he feels accepts him with his fears and insecurities and is open and honest with her own.

Our healing journey involves recognizing how we live in compensation and being willing to explore and expose our shamed-self.

Exercise:

Take a moment to reflect on your usual behavior, particularly with other people:

- In what way do you feel this behavior may not feel authentic or in tune with your soul?

- How does it feel inside when you are acting in this way?

- What specific behaviors do you feel might be compensations?

- What do you think you are covering up with this behavior?

CHAPTER 4:

THE SHAMED-SELF

When we begin to explore our shame, we have moved to the second floor.

We are ready to begin to explore our shamed-self and how it shows itself. As shame is a deep hypnosis, a trance that is covering our true essence, it can be very helpful to explore it according to the three ways we have already described—how we *feel when shame takes over,* how we *think,* and how we *behave* when we are in shame.

Let's take a look at Marco's story. As a child, he was teased continually by his brother Leonardo, who was two years older. Leonardo called him names like "stupid," "ugly," and "useless," but at the same time, he protected Marco from being bullied at school by other students. As a result, Marco adored Leonardo, even though he was regularly humiliated by him. He grew up in his older brother's shadow, copied him, and tried to be just like him in every way. He wanted to wear the same clothes; talk and act like him, and be with his friends.

Deep inside, Marco felt inferior and doubted his ability to do anything well. He developed a self-image that he was "second best," and whenever he and his brother would compete with each other in sports, as they often did, he would nearly always lose. He began to expect to lose, and this expectation carried over to his competing with other people in sports as well. But he never stopped trying. Each new competition or trial became a test of his worth as a person.

As he grew older, this deep inner sense of inferiority caused him to become terrified whenever he had to take a test at school or compete in any way. Sometimes the fear was so great that he would give up inside before the trial was over. He could not forgive himself for being "inadequate." Even when it came to girls, he felt inferior to his brother and doubted how any girl he found attractive and sexy could be interested in him.

In spite of his insecurity and fears, Marco managed to perform well in his life. He was successful at school, became a doctor, and found himself reasonably attractive to women. But still, inside, he felt inadequate, and his self-worth would easily tumble with the slightest failure, setback, or rejection. He continued to rely on his brother for advice and was profoundly influenced whenever his brother criticized or questioned his judgment.

Then one day, after he had graduated from medical school and was working as a family physician, he went to a seminar on self-worth. The teacher was talking about something called, "shame," and he realized that this was what he had been feeling all his life. But he never knew what it was. His sense was that even though he was always trying so hard to be better, inside, he knew he was going to fail. He just wanted to hide. Sometimes, he felt that his whole struggle to prove himself was too hard and too much. But at the same time, he felt and still feels that if he could not prove that he could succeed at something, his life had no worth.

Learning about shame was such a relief for Marco because for the first time, he realized that his feeling had a name, that other people suffered from the same feelings that he did, and that this feeling of unworthiness was not his nature; it had a cause. He had a reason for feeling this way. He also learned at this seminar that shame is a false sense of self that is the result of negative conditioning.

This shamed-self often drives our lives, and the experience of shame can crush us.

It is universal.

The question is whether we are in touch with shame or not.

Sometimes, particularly after a significant rejection or failure, it becomes worse and can last for a long time.

The length of time it lasts depends on how deep our shame is.

We all have it, but it varies in its intensity from one person to another, depending on many factors—some of which are obvious, as we will describe.

But sometimes it is not so clear why one person is so stricken by shame and another person has an easier time dealing with it.

We are often asked, "What is the point of exploring shame? Does it not become worse if we give it our attention? And then, is it not never ending? Why not just ignore it and get on with our lives?"

These are very good questions.

But unless we embrace and explore our shame, it will show itself in indirect ways, and sooner or later, it will attack us when we least expect it.

If we reject a part of us, it will prevent us from being real, and that in turn will make it impossible to have a fulfilling life and have deep connections with people.

In truth, all of us have tremendous potential and incredible gifts.

But we also have deep fears and insecurities.

If we try to live our potential and realize our gifts by pushing over our insecurity, our life will always have a quality of unreality and violence in it.

Yet by learning to explore and accept the part of us that carries shame, we become real, deep, compassionate, and sensitive.

We can realize our gifts and experience love in a totally different way than if we were trying to live by pushing through our insecurities.

We can uncover a beautiful, unique, creative being waiting to be discovered and expressed in a flowing and gentle way.

Marco considers that this seminar was a turning point in his life. It took him on a journey of healing his shame that involved attending many other seminars together with participating in individual therapy, exploring the roots of his insecurity, how he compromised and invalidated himself over the years, and finally coming to discover who he was different from his older brother. Today, he is even grateful for the shame he went through because he feels that it made him a deeper and more sensitive person. And his relationship with his brother has totally changed. Now they are truly friends, each with his own area of expertise, achievement, and pride. They respect each other immensely, and they realize how profoundly similar they are in spite of their differences, partly because they have come out of the same early shame conditioning.

Exercise:

Observe how it feels inside when you are having a shame attack.

- How does it affect your energy?

- What body sensations are you aware of?

- How does this feeling affect your thinking about yourself and your behavior?

CHAPTER 5:

SHAME THINKING

Shame comes with definite negative beliefs that we carry about ourselves and life.

Have you ever considered how strong these judgments are and how much they control your life?

In this chapter, we are going to guide you to take a better look at your judgments and how they come up.

They are beliefs based on a sense of separation, pain, and mistrust. Here is what can provoke shame thoughts:

- When we experience a *failure or a rejection* or when we anticipate a failure or a rejection

- When we are in a *social situation* like a party that makes us feel insecure

- When we are in an *unfamiliar environment,* when we move to a new place or country, or when we do something new

- When we have to *take a test,* apply for *a new job,* or have an interview for a new job

- After we have been in a social situation with one or more people and we judge ourselves mercilessly for *saying and doing stupid things,* trying to impress someone, or not saying the "right" things

- When we are in a social environment with people whom we find attractive and we *compare ourselves* to others whom we think are more attractive than we are

- When we face a *difficult challenge* in our lives, start or end a relationship, or take on bigger responsibilities at work

- When we see *another person's success* and compare ourselves to that person

Sometimes we might not hear the shame voices clearly, but they can cripple our energy, causing us to become depressed, collapse, and be easily overwhelmed.

When shame takes over, it means that us believe the shame voices.

For transformation to happen, it is important to begin to actually hear what the voices are saying to get some distance from the voices.

When we hear the voices clearly, we can question whether what they say is actually true or not.

However, the problem of shame is deeper than these negative beliefs that torment us or the crushing feeling inside that shame creates.

The problem is that these beliefs and this feeling about ourselves are so deeply ingrained in our psyche that they have created a *sense of self,* a deep *shame-based identity,* that we are a defective, deficient person who is incapable, unlovable, wrong, and bad.

We believe that we are this shamed-based identity.

That is why we call it "the shamed-self."

And when our identity is shame-based, the shame sticks to us like superglue.

Our beliefs and the feelings they bring strengthen our sense of ourselves as a shamed person.

Many of us have taken up residence on the middle floor.

We believe the shame voices in our heads that tell us that we are not good enough. And every new failure, criticism, judgment, or rejection fortifies these negative beliefs.

They become beliefs that control our lives and decide our actions.

Pedro is an accomplished guitar player and singer/songwriter. His deepest longing has always been to become a successful performer and to be able to live off his music. He is a gifted and successful psychologist, but his real love is his music. Unfortunately, he suffers from terrible stage fright, and when he performs in front of people, his hands shake so badly that he cannot play. As a child, he was not supported in his music. His parents considered that his music was just a hobby and felt that his efforts should be focused on becoming a doctor. He recalled that when he gave his first concert as a fourteen-year-old, neither of his parents bothered to come, and they did not even ask him how it went. Deep inside, he strongly believes that the world will never support him just as his parents never did. He is convinced that no matter what he does, he will never get the support he so longs for.

Helena has been in a relationship with an aggressive, abusive man for over five years. She was attracted to him because he was "strong" and made her feel attractive and desirable. When she was afraid or overwhelmed, she liked the secure feeling when he held her and would quickly forget all the times when he abused her verbally and sometimes physically. Her relating is controlled by the belief that this is the best she can do and that she is lucky to at least have someone who loves her.

Susanna is unhappy because she is desperately "in love" with a man who is not available for the kind of relationship she would like. He calls her from time to time; they go out and end the evening with what she describes as the most wonderful lovemaking she has ever experienced. Then for days, and sometimes weeks, she hears nothing from him. He claims that he is not into a committed relationship and prefers to date several women. He is happy with this arrangement and is not motivated to change. When she explores her controlling beliefs, she discovers that deep inside, she doesn't feel worthy of having the love of a man who is strong, self-reliant, and attractive. Even though she knows intellectually that this relationship is not healthy for her and that he will not change, she cannot extract herself.

The beliefs of the shamed-self will dominate our decision-making, our choices, and our behavior *until we begin to bring awareness to these beliefs and begin to question them.*

Let's explore some of your strong beliefs in specific aspects of your life. Think about whether you ever have thoughts like the ones listed below.

In relation to *work, money, and creativity,* do you believe that:

- "I will never make it."

- "I am not good enough and never will be."

- "I am lazy, and I don't put my whole energy into what I do."

- "I don't deserve to earn so much when others are suffering."

- "I don't really have anything special to offer."

In relation to *relationships, love, and sex,* do you believe that:

- "I am too much—too selfish, too loud, too alive, too sexual, too angry, too demanding, etc."

- "I am unattractive and boring."

- "I am not alive enough and much too repressed."

- "No one will ever love me."

- "It's not safe to trust anyone."

- "No one understands me."

- "If I open to someone, I will be taken advantage of."

- "If I open up, I will lose myself or I will lose my freedom."

- "I shouldn't be so needy."

In relation to your *body,* do you believe that:
- "I will always be fat."

- "I hate my breasts, my hips, my legs, etc."

- "I will never be in shape."

- "I am too old."

In relation to yourself as a *parent,* do you believe that:
- "I am too weak/too severe."

- "I made too many mistakes."

- "I don't/didn't love my child/children enough."

Naturally, when you hear some of these beliefs, you might immediately say, "But this is true!"

Yes, the sentence might have some truth in it, but a negative belief does not just stand alone as a statement of truth.

It carries a charge of condemning negativity.

And that negative charge crushes us. It kills our life energy, instead of supporting us so we can grow and learn.

Later in this handbook, we will teach you how to transform the negative judgments into an opportunity to grow.

But for now, we are simply helping you to identify your shame voices—your harsh self-judgments or judgments of others and life.

Exercise:

- Take a moment to see if you can identify the voices in your head when you experience or have experienced a failure or a rejection.

- These voices may be there all the time, but usually they become much louder and more troublesome when you suffer a setback.

- Write them down.

- Put a number next to each statement from 1–10 according to how much you believe this voice to be true (10 as the highest).

- Notice how this voice affects your energy and your behavior.

CHAPTER 6:

SHAME BEHAVIOR

Now let's take a look at the behavior that comes directly from a space of shame.

When we are in shame, it not only affects how we feel and think, it also affects how we act and the choices and decisions we make.

We call this "shame behavior."

Shame behavior is not the same as compensations because when we are compensating, we are trying to avoid shame.

With shame behavior, we are driven to behave in the ways described below because the shame compels us to act in this way.

It is shame-driven behavior.

Anna still compares herself to her younger sister. She always felt that her sister was prettier, more intelligent, and more sociable than she was. It seemed to her that her parents preferred her sister to her, and as a result, she was continually trying to prove herself to them. She excelled in school and became a successful basketball player. She won a scholarship to a prestigious college based on her skills as an athlete, but in spite of her accomplishments, she still felt inferior to her sister in the eyes of her parents. Whenever she is at home, she compulsively tries to impress her parents with her accomplishments.

Comparison is one of the most toxic shame-driven behaviors.

It is compulsive to compare when we are in shame. Whether we come out on top or on the bottom, it is the same.

Comparison is driven by the idea that our worth is based on an outside standard.

Adrian was applying to a prestigious medical school that he'd set his heart on attending. When he went for the interview, he was hoping to impress the doctor who was conducting the interview, but he was also extremely nervous and insecure. When he arrived, he noticed that a video camera was set up to record the interview. As he walked in, he accidentally tripped over the cord to the camera, causing it to crash to the floor and break. Feeling so guilty for what he had done, he walked out of the room without even beginning the interview.

Often our insecurity and shame can cause us to *sabotage, quit, or not even start* something that we really want.

Small setbacks or disappointments can easily convince us that we might as well give up.

Victor always feels awkward with women, especially if he is at-tracted sexually. He judges himself to be "a computer geek" and not a "sexy guy," and also believes that he is boring and has nothing to say of any interest. Recently, he found himself attracted to a woman at work. He found the courage to ask her out, and to his astonishment, she agreed. But once together, he felt awkward, shy, and inarticulate. He tried to make conversation, but it felt forced. At dinner, he kept drinking more and more glasses of wine in the hope that this would relax him and make him more interesting, but it only made him feel sick. At the end of the dinner, he had to excuse himself and vomited in the men's room. He was not surprised when she rejected his invitations for a second date. Inside, he had already anticipated that he would be rejected.

Our shame feelings of inadequacy in social situations, particularly if we are attracted to the person we are with, can cause us *to say and do things that we really don't want to do or say*, but we can't control ourselves.

The shame voices tell us that there is no reason why this person would like us or find us attractive, sexy, or interesting.

With this kind of belief, we create rejection.

Because of our shame, we may find ourselves in a relationship with someone who is disrespectful and even abusive and be unable to set a limit or to leave.

Helena accepts the abuse of her boyfriend because she feels that perhaps he is right, and she does deserve to be called selfish and stupid. It does not even occur to her to *set a limit* with this kind of treatment because in her shame, she does not feel she has the right to be treated kindly and with respect. She feels lucky to have her boyfriend in spite of his aggressive behavior. Also when he has not called her for several days, she calls him, even though she knows she is *acting like a beggar.* She says that she cannot control herself.

This kind of shame behavior can be a repeat, in some ways, of how we were treated as a child. But even if we know our childhood history, we may still find ourselves *attracted to partners who mistreat us.* We accept the disrespect and cannot find the courage or even the idea of setting a limit. Even worse, we *humiliate ourselves.*

It is as if our attractions are betraying us.

Often, it never even occurs to us that we could stand up for ourselves because we don't realize we are being mistreated.

When we have been repeatedly neglected or disrespected, we develop a deep inner belief that this is how life is, this is how we will always be treated, and this is how we deserve to be treated.

One of the most troublesome ways that we behave when we are in shame is to be attracted to and *to be in relationships with someone who is not emotionally available.*

Susan shows this kind of shame-based behavior. She is attracted, infatuated, and desperately in love with someone who is not really interested in having more than a casual friendly and sexual connection with her.

We do this "shame shopping" because unconsciously we are looking for someone who will validate us as a person or as a man or woman.

Our attraction is based on picking someone who meets an idea of who we would like to be.

In other words, we are saying to ourselves, "If I were the kind of man or woman I think I should be, this is the kind of man or woman who would be attracted to me." (Paradoxically, if we knew and accepted ourselves as we are, we probably would not even be attracted to this kind of person.)

In these situations, we will invariably be rejected because we are not coming to the person from a space of feeling valuable, lovable, attractive, or interesting.

We are coming with the opposite feelings and beliefs inside— feelings and beliefs of shame, of not being good enough.

It is like a movie script where the outcome is already predictable.

The other person picks up this self-deprecating vibration and responds according to our script.

Nathan admits that he has always been obsessed with what other people think of him. His focus is never on himself. When he is out with his friends, he is always thinking about how he is fitting in, if his friends like him, and if they include him as "one of the gang." He feels that many times, he *says something to impress* the other guys, but instead of getting their approval and respect, he gets the opposite. He often becomes the object of their jokes and feels humiliated. After the evening, he feels terrible and suffers a horrible shame attack convinced that he is boring, talks too much, and says stupid, uninteresting things.

A big part of shame is that we are *obsessively concerned about what other people think.*

Unfortunately, when our attention is not with ourselves, we are out of our center, and any behavior that comes from that space will be shame-based behavior that will make the shame feelings worse.

Exercise:

As you observe your life, can you catch yourself behaving in any of the ways we have described?

- Is it difficult for you *to set limits?*

- Do you find yourself *saying things just to impress or get attention?*

- Do you find *yourself being attracted to people who don't value or see you?*

- Do you find yourself in relationships with *people who disrespect you?*

- Do you find yourself *isolating yourself* because of shyness or insecurity?

- Do you find yourself *not starting something or not expressing yourself* because you are afraid of failure, criticism, humiliation, judgment, or rejection?

- Do you *quit* easily when you get discouraged?

- Do you find yourself *begging for love* or attention?

CHAPTER 7:

THE REAL-SELF

I f we are willing to connect and explore our shamed-self on the middle floor, the bottom floor will open naturally.

It may not seem that way at first, but the journey toward wholeness begins by exploring the middle floor of the shamed-self and ends on the bottom floor of the real-self.

Let's begin by exploring how the real-self develops and matures as we age.

A young child has a basic and essential need for guidance and support.

But even more importantly, a young child has a basic need to be seen and recognized.

It is very rare for us as children to know who we are.

Without guidance, we get distracted from our beings and start following other people's agendas that have nothing to do with who we are—agendas such as parental and cultural expectations, religious and moral beliefs, and standards of success that are put into our young and innocent minds, preventing us from discovering and developing our own truth.

These agendas condition us to become who and what we are not.

If we satisfy these expectations, we have lost ourselves, and if we fail to satisfy them, we are shamed.

Without the love, recognition, and appreciation of "the big people" for who we are and can become, we lose touch with our authentic selves.

That is how shame is created.

There are, of course, many parents who recognize the gifts of their child or children and may even make incredible sacrifices to support their child to develop his or her gifts.

But unfortunately, these are exceptions and are most often the case when a child's gifts are extraordinary. We all have gifts, to be sure, but they may not stand out so clearly; if so, we are much more vulnerable to negative conditioning.

In truth, we are utterly unique, and we have something so special and precious to express, to give, and to contribute to the world.

The potential is there, the impulses are there, but for this potential to become actualized, it needs to be recognized by a parent, teacher, or a therapist who sees and feels it and can help cultivate it.

Unfortunately, most parents and teachers are not tuned in to our uniqueness.

They have an idea, a prewritten script for us, and their efforts are directed toward having us fulfill this script.

If we are very strong, we might resist this repressive pressure and rebel.

But most children do not have this kind of inner knowing to rebel, and even if they do, most often their healthy rebelliousness is squashed or becomes self-destructive.

It takes a lot of courage to begin to investigate and discover our truth and to question what we were taught; to begin to move from the shamed-self to our real-self. To encourage that process, it is necessary for us to separate emotionally, physically, and psychologically from our family of origin to find ourselves. Later, once the process has matured, we can re-connect with our family from a totally new and different space.

With courage, commitment, and guidance we can rediscover our real-self.

We may have some glimpses of this part of us when we are being creative, dancing, engaging in some kind of sports, making love, being with a child or an animal, or giving care and love to someone.

In those moments, we have an authentic experience of being in flow with the beauty of life, perhaps expressing our unique talents, opening our heart, and finding a space of inner peace.

In these moments, our motivation does not come from needing the appreciation and approval of others, but from living in tune with what we know in our deepest soul to be true.

The dramas or peaks and valleys of emotion disappear, and life feels remarkably ordinary, simple, and natural.

Then, in the next moment, that wonderful space disappears, and we find ourselves back in the shamed-self, full of self-doubt and worries.

The goal of this journey is to make the experience of the real-self last more than just a fleeting moment.

The goal is to find a deeper, more consistent, and more reliable sense inside of ourselves that feels authentic and flowing and to become aware that the experience of shame—the shamed identity—is false.

The shamed-self is not who we are.

It is helpful for us to begin to recognize what it feels like when we are back home in our real-self.

There is a sense of ease and flow in the body, a lightness, and a joy.

Exercise:

1. Can you recall a time recently when you felt flowing, alive, in tune with life and yourself?

    *   What were you doing at the time?

    *   How did this experience feel inside?

    *   What kinds of thoughts did or might you have had at this time?

2. What kinds of behavior can you identify that help you connect with your real self?

3. What people in your life may support you being in your real self?

    *   What is it about these people that help you feel this way?

    *   What do they do or say (or not do and say) that helps you feel this way?

CHAPTER 8:

THE CAUSES OF SHAME

When we feel shame, most often we believe "this is who I am, I have always been this way and I will never be any different."

In the moments that we get overtaken by shame, we are not aware of any other reality.

When we develop a shame identity, we cannot imagine that shame is a state of being that happened to us. We truly believe we were born this way.

We were not.

A child does not suffer from crippling insecurity, unreasonable fears, and lack of inspiration and confidence.

All of that comes as a result of our surroundings and upbringings, and it happens to each of us in different ways.

The specific way in which we were shamed is *our shame story*.

One crucial step on our journey of healing shame is knowing our shame story—knowing and feeling how we were humiliated and distracted from being ourselves. (This process is not to blame or vilify our parents or teachers but simply to see things as they were with clarity and insight. Most often our caretakers did the best they could but nonetheless, unconsciousness causes shame.)

As we continue educating you more about shame, we invite you to ask yourself some deep and important questions:

- Can you remember times in your childhood and adolescence when you felt humiliated by your parents, teachers, or other children?

- Did you feel welcomed into your family as a child, did your parents spend time with you, or did one or both parents leave you?

- Can you remember ways that your parents disrespected your privacy?

- Did someone beat you as a child?

- As a child, did an adult overtly invade you sexually or with suggestions and teasing?

- Did your parents put strong pressure and expectations on you?

- Did your parents expect you to become something that they thought was important but was not in tune with who you were?

- Were you conditioned to play a certain role in your family such as caretaker, clown, hero, high achiever, or the one people felt sorry for?

- Were you subjected to strict and rigid rules or religious conditioning as a child?

- Were you not given clear and loving limits?

- Were there family secrets?

- Was one or both of your parents addicted to alcohol or drugs?

- Do you remember being criticized or compared to someone else?

All of these questions point to the ways you might have been shamed.

We now are going to take a little time to go through the most significant causes of shame in childhood. Some of the items on this list may not have been your experience, but as you read though them, see and feel which ones apply to your childhood experiences.

1. Humiliation

One of the most common causes of shame is humiliation.

We are exquisitely sensitive beings. If our integrity is not respected, we develop a sense of ourselves as someone who does not deserve respect. From this sense of ourselves, we will invite continual disrespect later in our life.

As a child and teenager, we could have been humiliated in many ways. The stories of Alicia and Michael, below, illustrate some common childhood humiliations.

Alicia has always had trouble with being overweight. She was overweight as a child, as a teenager, and now as an adult. Her mother shamed her for her weight and told her that men do not like fat women, and unless she lost her extra weight, she would never find a man who loves her. Her mother continually pressured her to diet, forcing her to attempt different weight-loss regimens including taking diet pills. All this humiliation and pressure had the opposite effect on her of gaining more weight and feeling worse about herself. Alicia's overeating was clearly a symptom of the anxiety she felt for being so scrutinized by her mother plus the continual conflicts in the home between her parents. But there was no one to explain this to her, and she blamed herself for not being able to lose weight and for her parents fighting.

We might have been humiliated by being bullied at home or in school. Perhaps we may remember experiences as a child in school when we felt isolated from the "in crowd," or were teased by other students or shamed by a teacher in front of the class.

This happened to Michael. He was teased for being small for his age and shy. Michael felt too ashamed to mention this to his parents, but at the age of seven, he began to stutter badly. This handicap only made the bullying worse. He judged himself harshly because he could not stand up to the boys who bullied him. He had no one to talk to, kept all the pain inside, and went deeper and deeper into feelings of unworthiness and inadequacy.

2. *Pressure, Expectations, and Comparison*

It is also humiliating if our parents and culture use pressure, expectations, and comparison to force us to become someone or achieve something. Often these expectations have nothing to do with us.

As a child, we needed support to find our own passion in life. We needed for "the big people" to be so attuned to us that they could see and encourage our gifts and our passions. But if the adults in our life do not support us in pursuing our own interests, it can be a humiliating experience, as Christian's story shows.

Christian was raised by a strict father who expected him to perform up to his high standards. If Christian did not bring home top grades in school, his father punished him by not talking to him for days. He wanted him to become a doctor like he was, and he considered all other professions inferior. Christian actually studied medicine to win his father's approval, but his heart was never in it. His passion was to become a carpenter and create specialized furniture. Eventually, he found the courage to quit medicine and follow his dream, but inside, he felt he had let his father down. He was still carrying his father's values, and so he still couldn't fully enjoy and feel proud of his new profession.

3. *Physical and Emotional Abuse*

It is now well known that any kind of physical abuse to a child is profoundly shaming.

Children only understood love, and naturally attempt to bond in love with their parents.

But if children are the target of violence from one or both of their parents, it is hopelessly confusing.

Then the child asks him- or herself, "How can someone who loves me also inflict physical pain on me?"

The only way children can make sense of abuse from their parents is to blame themselves and come to believe that they deserve to be treated in this way—as happened with Dominic, below.

Dominic was deeply frightened of his father because of his anger and his habit of exploding and shouting. At the table, his father ridiculed him when he shared about his fears and insecurities at school and often told him that he needed to stop acting like such a girl. Still, Dominic desperately wanted his father's approval and love. When his father was working in the garage, he would go to him and ask if he could help him. When his father gave him a chore to do, his father would become impatient and hit him. Once his father asked him to fetch a screwdriver, but when Dominic brought back a different one than the one his father wanted, his father hit him in the face with it.

Dominic came to feel that he was not capable of doing anything right. His fear of authority has stayed with him, and he judges himself as being "such a wimp." In many ways, his father crushed Dominic's will.

When we hear such a story, we may feel anger and pain for this little boy. But it is easy to forget how often our own will, curiosity, enthusiasm, and joy were crushed by ridicule, rules, or violence.

4. *Sexual Abuse*

Clearly, if a child is sexually abused by an adult, this is one of the most shaming experiences any child can experience.

Sexual abuse includes not only actual sexual acts from an adult toward a child, but also any incidents when an adult looks at a child with sexual desire, treats the child as a sexual object, or makes sexual comments or jokes.

Although many people minimize or deny how much shame this causes, the humiliation and damaging consequences of this kind of trauma is overwhelming. Andrea's story demonstrates how harmful and long-lasting the effects can be.

Andrea's father began abusing her sexually when she was five and continued for five years. He told her that it was a secret between them and not to tell her mother. In her teenage years, Andrea distanced herself from her parents, became sexually active when she was thirteen, and moved out of the house to live on her own when she was sixteen. She knew that the abuse had happened, but she felt she had put the experience behind her. She dressed provocatively and had little trouble attracting men. She didn't think that she had any trouble with her sex life. But after she had been married for three years, something changed. Her husband began to feel intimidated by her sexual aggression and insecure that he could not meet her strong sexual needs. This problem brought them into therapy, and Andrea was persuaded to begin working with healing the abuse. She began to discover how deeply she judged her body and her sexuality. She felt dirty and hated herself for having felt aroused when her father had touched her. She also felt that she had betrayed her mother. It helped her to know and understand that she was feeling classic symptoms of abuse and that it would take time to heal.

5. *Invasion of a Child's Natural Freedoms*

It is also shaming when a parent invades a child's space, reads his or her diary, is possessive or controlling, and interferes in the child's private life.

Every person needs to discover and develop *essential freedoms*— the freedom to think, feel, intuit, dream, and believe what he or she wants to believe.

A healthy parent will encourage his or her child to develop these freedoms.

We are deeply shamed when, instead of being supported, beliefs are crammed down our throat and we are told what to think, and what feelings and behavior are appropriate.

The result is that we will lose these freedoms and no longer know or trust our own thoughts, feelings, intuition, behavior, and beliefs.

Perhaps you can reflect on how these five freedoms were repressed and unsupported in your childhood. What were you told to think and believe? How was your spontaneity crushed? Were your feelings supported or shamed? Or perhaps some were supported and others not?

6. *Neglect*

As a child, we need to feel welcomed into our family as a special and unique person. And once here, we need time and care that is especially devoted to us.

If, however, we feel that our parents do not have time or interest in receiving us, feel burdened taking care of our early needs, don't spend time with us, and don't help us to discover and feel our uniqueness, we begin to shrink inside.

Or if we are one of many children so that the time devoted to us alone is diluted and generalized to all the children, this can also become abusive neglect. We may start to become a beggar for love and attention. This is something that feels deeply humiliating and creates trouble in future relationships.

Such is the case with Suzanna. She was the last of six children; her father was rarely at home, and her mother was overburdened with her role as the only caretaker. Suzanna cannot remember having quality time with either of her parents. Her experience of her father is absence, and of her mother, stress and anxiety. In her relationships in general and with men specifically, she minimizes her needs, apologizes for feeling or wanting anything for herself, and has developed the personality of someone who is always "there for other people." But inside, she feels that she is invisible, and that is precisely how she felt as a child.

7. Being Conditioned to Play a Role

It is equally humiliating if we were conditioned to play a role in the family.

We will start to believe that our worth as a person depends on fulfilling that role.

We may have become the *caretaker* or *the responsible one* in our family.

Perhaps we stepped in as the caretaker for a depressed parent or for our brothers and sisters or the family because a parent or parents were irresponsible or abusing alcoholic or other substances.

As a caretaker, we come to believe that our value as a person depends on helping people and taking care of things.

Not only is it a terrible burden, but also people resent being taken care of. And believing that our self worth depends on caretaking will have a profound effect on all our future relationships.

Perhaps we became *the clown*, a role we adopt because trying to be funny and the object of jokes becomes a way of getting attention.

It is basically a compensation for feeling like a failure.

Or we might have taken on the role of the *hero* or the *high achiever*.

Then our love and respect as a person becomes dependent on successes and diplomas.

In a world where achievements generally have the highest value, it is so easy to slip into the high achiever role and forget that our value never depends on what we do.

We live under the constant stress that we may disappoint ourselves or someone else.

And perhaps the most shaming role of all is that of the *victim or the irresponsible child*.

We may have adopted this role because we felt inside that we could not keep up with what was expected of us.

Our way of dealing with this constant pressure and anxiety was simply to give up inside.

Since we lost hope of getting love and attention the positive way by proving our value, we turned to getting negative attention by being sick, or by getting people to feel sorry for us.

As a victim, we regard everything as a problem, we complain constantly, and blame others and the world for our unhappiness.

This role is deeply humiliating, but when we have been playing it for a long time, it is difficult to drop it.

We may also have started playing this role as a way of bonding with a parent who was in the role of the victim.

The problem with all of these roles is that we have become identified with them. And once we believe that this is who we are, we have lost ourselves.

8. *Excessive or Absence of Limits*

As a child, we need a healthy balance of freedom and limits. It is no easy task for parents to strike a balance between flexible boundaries and discipline and guidance. But either extreme is deeply shaming. Too rigid rules will stifle developing our creativity and individuality but no or unreliable limits can cause us to feel that we are a boat floating aimlessly in the sea.

9. *Being Infected with Negativity, Depression, or Shame*

The last cause of shame that we want to mention is being infected with the shame, depression, or negativity of a parent, as happened to Maria, below.

Maria's mother was chronically depressed and on two occasions, she tried unsuccessfully to kill herself by taking sleeping pills. One of those times, Maria found her mother and saved her by rushing her to the hospital. She was deeply conflicted inside because on the one hand, she felt that she loved her mother and wanted to try to make her happy, but on the other, she was furious at her and could even feel hate for her. She notices that she carries her mother's pessimism about life and feels that if she were really a "good" person, her mother would have been joyful and excited about life and about being her mother.

As a child, we can easily blame ourselves for all the sadness, conflict, and problems around us.

In this kind of environment, we feel deeply inside that we cause unhappy people around us to suffer if we are different or joyful.

We may also blame ourselves for the ways we did not live up to your parents' or society's expectations, or for not being attractive, intelligent, sensitive, alive, or compassionate enough.

Anger Can Be Healing

We often encounter in our work a tendency for people to feel that they would like or should forgive anyone who shamed them in their past. (Or even in the present.) This is a natural sentiment but if it is premature, it can sabotage our healing because first we have to feel how deeply we were shamed and have compassion for what we went through. And it is both natural and healthy to feel anger for what happened because it is simply not okay to treat children in the way that many of us were treated.

It is one of the ways we bring our self-love back.

It is healing to feel anger:

- For being treated in neglectful, disrespectful ways

- For being humiliated at a time when you could not defend yourself

- For having to play roles or become someone you are not

- For being raised by a parent who was not positive about life

- Or for being raised by people who hid behind repressive religious ideas

- Or for having parents who couldn't find healthy ways to deal with their own pain, fear, and disappointments

The anger can help us break through the deadness and the numbness and help us wake up and come fully alive.

It is not healthy to stay angry or to blame our parents, teachers, or religious authority figures for how they might have shamed us. But we can use the energy of anger as fuel to wake up our life energy, and to help us discover our truth.

And it can help to realize that we are angry at the behavior but not at the person.

People often ask us how to find meaning in life.

The three qualities that bring meaning to life are:

- Discovering joy in being alive

- Contributing from our own special passion and creativity

- And most importantly, finding people to share our love with

To enjoy these three qualities, we must first recover a space in which we appreciate ourselves.

Exercise:

To bring your shame story into your awareness, take a moment to review the causes we have mentioned above.

Can you relate to any of these causes of shame from your life, especially as a child?

1. Humiliation

2. Violence

3. Sexual abuse or other forms of invasion

4. Pressure and expectations

5. Being conditioned to live a certain life and have a certain profession

6. Neglect and absence of support

7. Adopting a role in the family

8. Infected with the negativity or depression of a parent

9. Strict rules or religious conditioning

10. Being overprotected

CHAPTER 9:

FEELING THE SHAME

I t is important to know our shame story and recall shaming experiences from our past.

But it is not enough to just know about them.

We also have to feel them.

Quite often, when people know how they were shamed and humiliated, they may think that the work is over and now they can get on with their lives.

But the impact of shame is deep and does not heal just by having an intellectual awareness of it.

One essential factor that helps us to heal and come out of our shame identity is when we can re-experience these traumatic events now with the awareness, resources, and strength of an adult looking and feeling back to what it was really like for us when it happened.

When we think back on the ways we were shamed in the ways we have mentioned, often we may do it with a certain detachment—almost as though it was not us who went through these experiences.

It is important for us to feel the impact of what happened to us from the perspective of a young, innocent, helpless, vulnerable, and trusting child.

Until we do that, we will continue to be unkind and critical toward ourselves or others in the same way that we were treated as a child.

There are two ways that we can connect directly with the feeling of being shamed.

One way is to recall an event from our past that was especially humiliating and then imagine that it is our child (if we have a child) or any child who is experiencing this trauma.

- How would that feel for this child?

- How would it make this child feel about him- or herself?

- How would it affect his or her trust and self-confidence?

The other way is to recall the same or a similar event and imagine ourselves back in time when we were that age.

Then ask ourselves the same questions:

- How would that feel if we imagine ourselves as a child?

- How would it make us feel about ourselves at this time?

- How would it affect our trust and self-confidence?

It is much safer to consider our shaming experiences intellectually. It is more risky to allow ourselves to actually feel how it was for us. There are many possible feelings that this exercise can provoke.

- We might feel humiliation—a feeling that makes we want to hide and makes us feel small and sick.

- We might feel shock—a feeling of frozenness and lack of emotions.

- We might feel sadness or anger that we were mistreated in this way.

Exercise:

(We feel we should suggest some caution with this exercise because it may provoke strong emotions. It would be good to do it when you feeling strong and centered inside rather than when you are experiencing a difficult time.)

Take a moment to recall a specific moment in your childhood when you remember feeling humiliated, abused, ignored, or compared to.

Pick one incident that stands out for you as being particularly difficult or painful.

Imagine yourself going back in time and find yourself back at the time that this incident happened.

At the same time, be aware that you are now much stronger and did survive that event, so you can feel it now and bring awareness to how it affected you.

Allow yourself to picture the whole scene—picture all the people who are present at this time and where they are in relation to where you are in this scene.

Now, hear and see the shaming words or actions and see who is doing or saying them.

Let yourself feel just how it must have felt to this little boy/girl at the time that this happened.

- How does this child feel inside?

- What happens to his or her energy?

- How does the child feel about him- or herself?

- What does the child judge about him- or herself?

- How does the child feel toward the person or persons who are doing this?

CHAPTER 10:

THE POWER OF AWARENESS

So far, we have explored shame compensations, how shame feels, what we think when we are in shame, and how we act from shame, and the shame story—how we were shamed.

From our exploration so far, you may see how your shame self-image has run your life, and you have gone back to feel the impact of this shaming.

Now we are ready to learn the practical tools of transforming shame in our daily lives.

The first aspect of this transformation process is learning how to be with shame when it comes up.

This is the power of awareness—of meditation. But not the kind of meditation that involves sitting silently (although that is also helpful).

This is the kind of meditation that means becoming an ever-present watcher who observes our feelings, thoughts, and actions.

We are going to apply that quality of awareness, of meditation, to learning to be with our shame.

The power of awareness is our ability to step back a little from ourselves and observe.

Normally, we might not do that.

Instead, we might go through our lives much like a robot on autopilot.

But as soon as we introduce a quality of witnessing, our lives transform.

Suddenly we have choice and freedom.

As we have seen, when we are in shame, it affects our bodily sensations, our emotions, thoughts, and behavior.

With awareness, we can now observe ourselves being in shame.

The Five Points of Awareness

We can observe the whole experience of shame and how it takes over our senses and our perception of reality.

First of all, we need to become aware that we are in shame.

Something has triggered us and we have entered into the hypnosis of shame.

This is *the first point of awareness.*

Sometimes we might notice that we are taken over by shame because of how it *feels in the body.*

This is *the second point of awareness.*

Our energy crashes, we lack motivation, we feel hopeless and negative about our life, about life in general, or we are feeling judgmental and negative about others or another person.

Or we might become aware that we are engaged in *shame-based behavior*—compromising, saying something we don't mean, exaggerating, bragging, lying, begging, rescuing, easily getting enraged, overeating or drinking, or distracting ourselves with pornography, TV, the Internet, or shopping.

This is *the third point of awareness.*

Finally, we might notice our negative thoughts. These could be directed toward ourselves, toward another, or toward life in general.

If we pay close attention, we may discover that these thoughts are habitual, automatic, and compulsive.

We may find ourselves believing them completely.

This is all part of shame.

But if we observe our negative thoughts from a certain distance, we might also slowly notice that they are not always present.

At times, we feel more optimistic about ourselves, others, and life.

But other times, when we are taken over by shame, we can notice how these negative thoughts take over.

Observing the shame thoughts *is the fourth point of awareness.*

The final point of awareness is to become conscious of what triggers our shame.

In summary, here are the five points of awareness:

- We notice *we are in a shame trance.*

- We notice how shame *feels* in our bodies.

- We notice how we *behave* when we are in shame.

- We notice the *negative thoughts* when we are taken over by shame.

- We become aware of what may have *triggered* our shame.

Now that we know a bit about our shame story, we know what kinds of things shamed us in the past.

When we experience something similar in our lives today, such as being criticized, judged, or rejected, failing, not doing something perfectly, starting something new, setting a limit, or taking some other kind of risk, most likely our shame will be triggered.

Our Shame Sensitivities

Sometimes we may not be able to directly connect what provoked our shame today to a past experience of being shamed.

But we may still be able to begin to understand what our shame triggers are because in more than one incident, similar situations brought on a shame attack.

We call these *"our shame sensitivities."*

Bringing this quality of awareness toward noticing that we are in shame, observing our body experience in shame, our shame behavior, and shame thoughts, and what triggers our shame, still misses one ingredient.

That quality is *acceptance*.

It means observing ourselves when we are in shame with compassion, with deep understanding, and with love.

A child has no option but to become shamed and no ability or resources to understand or avoid it.

As children, we felt we deserved to be treated this way, and we had no way to love ourselves when we were in shame.

Today, we can be with ourselves in a different way.

We invite you to observe yourself when you are in shame as if you are embracing a deeply wounded child, perhaps your own child (if you have one), who has come home from school feeling ashamed, insecure, or humiliated.

Allow your heart to embrace this shamed part of you, filling it with your love and understanding that it is a very deep, old, and a powerful way you have seen yourself and believed yourself to be.

Finally, it might help to say to yourself:

"This is the shamed part of me who has been through many shaming experiences in the past. I know that this is not all of me, nor is it who I really am, but right now it has taken over my consciousness. I am going to practice observing this part of me and giving it my love and understanding."

Exercise

Make a regular habit of becoming more aware when you are in shame.

The next time you notice you are taken over by insecurity, unworthiness, and feelings of inferiority and inadequacy, step back a bit and know that this is a wounded part of you.

Take yourself through the five points of awareness:

1. Notice that you are in shame.

2. Notice how it feels in the body.

3. Notice any shame-based behavior.

4. Notice any negative shame thoughts about yourself, others, or life.

5. Notice what may have triggered the shame.

Breathe your love into your shame.

CHAPTER 11:

CHANGING CHANNELS—HOW TO TAME OUR INNER JUDGE

When we are in shame, we are being attacked by our inner judge.

Sometimes it may seem that the provocation has come from someone's criticism or rejection, or from an event or situation, but inside our inner critic has taken over and is pouring judgments on us.

If we were not judging ourselves in this situation, then another person's judgments would not matter to us.

However, we may not be aware of the inner judge because we have internalized the judgments so deeply.

Part of the process of healing and recovering from shame is becoming aware of our inner judge and learning how to deal with it.

We all develop an inner judge because it helped and helps us deal with living in the real world.

In a positive sense, it gives us a way of establishing structure for ourselves, giving us guidelines, direction, and an ability to evaluate right from wrong.

But the judge is formed from the values, rules, convention, and fears of those who raise us and the society in which we live.

Its intention is not for us to live a full, energetic, adventuresome, and expansive life, but rather to help protect us so that we can fit in, be respected, and belong to the crowd.

Also, the judge often bases its opinion of us on how well we do in a competitive world.

Here is the problem with the judge:

- The rules of our judge *repress our life energy*.

- Our sense of ourselves becomes based on how well we please our judge or perform in *comparison to others*, and that creates constant stress.

- *Living for safety* alone and conforming to society's rules is deadening and does not help us develop our unique qualities, intelligence, and gifts.

- The standards our judge holds for us have little or *nothing to do with who we are*.

All of this alone would be terrible enough.

But to make it even worse, when we do have the courage to stray from the rules—when we don't conform, fail, get rejected, or try something new—the judge attacks us with a fury.

When we get an attack from our judge, we will experience powerful *fear* and *guilt* because these are the two tools the judge uses to keep us in line.

And in our shame, we believe the judge.

We don't even know that we are under attack; we just think we are wrong.

With some awareness, effort, and understanding, we can change this painful mechanism.

Part of the reason we believe our judge so strongly is because sometimes what it is saying sounds true on the surface.

For instance, if we are overweight, the judge says, "You are fat!"

The energy comes in a heartless, condemning way, and if we listen closely, it would probably go on to say, "You are also unattractive, lazy, undisciplined, and you will never get the love or respect you want."

This is just one example, but it is the same with any kind of shame attack we are going through.

Switching Channels

We would like to suggest a simple but effective way to tame and transform the attacks of our inner judge.

We call it "switching channels."

We are accustomed to listening to the channel of the harsh, critical, condemning, unloving judge.

We invite you to switch channels and listen to something very different.

This new channel we call "the loving energy."

Let's take the example from above.

Your judge says, "You are fat!" and then other judgments that follow from that.

The loving energy might say, "Yes, it is a fact that you weigh more than what you would like, and it feels uncomfortable for you.

"But most probably you have used food as a way of soothing your anxiety because of the pain, shame, and/or fear you carry from what happened to you in your past.

"But rather than condemn yourself for being overweight, understand that the relationship between food and your body is just a place where your trauma shows itself.

"Be gentle and loving with yourself, and with time, you will find other ways to soothe yourself.

"Let's begin by just paying attention to what it feels like to be in this body.

"Maybe we can take a little step to take a walk regularly to move some energy to help make it easier to feel the body.

"Let's find out what you are really longing for and missing."

The loving energy teaches us to feel and see ourselves in a loving way.

It teaches us to understand that the reason any of us do things that are not intelligent or healthy is only because we have pain, fear, and shame inside and we are trying to meet some very deep needs.

It teaches us that there is always another way that we can see ourselves and that way is from the heart, with deep love and understanding.

Since most of us were not taught to look at ourselves lovingly, we need to learn how to do so.

We were taught to listen to the judge, and this has become automatic

It takes practice and constant remembering to change from the channel of the judge to the channel of the loving energy.

Let's take another example.

You have taken an exam and you failed.

Most likely you failed because you did not prepare enough or you were so nervous when you took the exam that you couldn't concentrate, or you are not really interested in the subject, or you have a deep pattern of sabotaging yourself under pressure.

The judge says, "See how stupid you are! You did not even have enough intelligence to prepare for that test. And you are always like that!

You don't apply yourself. You are a failure because you just don't have what it takes to be successful in life. You behave like a child, and you expect other people to take care of you. It is time that you grow up!"

Now switch channels.

The loving energy might say, "Yes, you failed, and probably if you had taken longer to prepare, you would have done better. But it is clear that because of your shame, you sabotage yourself. That is what happens with shame. You have always felt so much pressure inside to be better—to compare yourself to others, to work hard and earn the respect of your family—that you give up just to relieve the stress inside. The more you discover and trust what you love to do, the easier you will find it is to do things better because your heart is in it. Keep learning to trust your own heart and let that guide you."

The loving energy embraces our difficulties with understanding and depth and finds a way to embrace whatever we are judging about ourselves in the light of compassion.

It will have a totally different effect on us than the attack of the judge.

Sometimes we may get so taken over by a judge attack and feel so deep in shame that we cannot get enough space to change channels.

In that case, we might try asking a trusted friend to be the loving energy for us and listen to what he or she might say.

Or we might take a walk in nature or dance or do whatever helps us feel the aliveness in our body.

One of essential aspects of having a healing relationship with a good therapist is that she will constantly reflect the loving energy back to us no matter what we are going through.

The same can happen in a functional intimate relationship when both partners have done individual work on their shame and are then able to understand each others' difficulties and set aside their own. (That is a tall order that we will address is a later volume of The Learning Love Handbook.)

Exercise 1:

The next time you notice that you are feeling shame and judging yourself, try the following steps:

1. Notice *what your judge is saying to you.*

2. *Feel the impact of this attack* and observe that the judgments are coming *without love* and not taking in your situation

3. *Tune in to your heart* and imagine that your heart is now seeing and feeling the whole situation.

4. (If you are unable to do this, *ask a friend* to be the loving energy.)

5. Notice what this heartful, *loving energy says to you.*

6. *Feel the difference* between this and the attack of the judge.

Exercise 2:

Write a letter to yourself from the loving energy, your inner wisdom.

Imagine that it knows you intimately and is able to give you the kind of support, guidance, and acceptance that most likely you missed as a child.

CHAPTER 12:

NEW THINKING, NEW CHOICES, NEW DECISIONS, AND NEW HABITS

W e now come to the final step of recovering from shame. Much of our self-esteem is based on how we live our lives—the thoughts we carry, the decisions we make, the actions we take, and the habits we follow.

Many of our thoughts, decisions, actions, and habits may have been or may still be based on shame. If so, we may live our lives in a cloud of negativity, much as Henry does:

Henry is a forty-five-year-old man whose relationship is in trouble because his wife is tired of his being "low energy, depressed, and negative." When we ask about this, he admits that often he gets into a "down mood" and has a hard time getting out of it. In these times, he loses a sense of meaning in life and sits around watching television or complaining. He learned this attitude and behavior from his father, and it has haunted him all his life. Henry has worked on his shame, he knows its roots, and he has explored his past and is in touch with the wounded part of him that holds this negativity. But he still gets lost in negative thinking that causes him to become depressed and collapsed. We have told him that it is now time for him to pay close attention to this negative thinking and take some concrete action steps to move out of it because negativity has become a safe and familiar hiding place for him.

First, we suggested that he bring awareness to the *negative thoughts and actually write them down.*

Second, we suggested that he begin to introduce *daily rituals* that allow him to feel good about himself such as starting the day with some exercise and a healthy breakfast.

Third, we suggested that he explore what gives his *life meaning* and make *some simple goals* in that direction.

Fourth, we invited him to take *some small steps* in the direction of these goals.

When we become acutely aware of our negative thinking and then take positive, concrete action toward living a more rewarding and meaningful life, this actually activates the "Yes toward Life" impulse inside all of us.

This "Yes" is a place inside that embraces life and knows embracing life is the truth. But it can get clouded over by our negative shame voices.

When we take action and move toward the positive, the clouds will slowly disappear.

Let's explore more deeply how negative shame thoughts have led or may still lead your life.

What decisions have you made in your life based on shame?

Your shame *decisions* may be or have been:

- To be attracted to or enter into a relationship with someone who is not available or is abusive

- To be in an unfulfilling or abusive relationship and be unable to end it

- To choose a career or do work that is not right for you

- To choose a place to live that is not right for you

What *actions* do you have that are coming from shame? They may include:

- To receive disrespect without being able to stand up for yourself

- To make love in ways that was or is not right for you

- To compulsively seek other's opinions about your life and to listen to these opinions rather than to learn to listen to your own wisdom.

- To quit something as soon as you get disappointed or have a little setback

- Not to start something because it seems too difficult

- To say something that you do not want to say

- To compulsively seek attention

- To be dishonest

- To exaggerate to impress people

- To spend more money that you make or can afford

- To have unfinished emotional business with people and not take action to clean it up

What *habits* do you have that are shame based?

- To eat or overeat food that is not healthy or nourishing.

- Not to exercise or to exercise too much without listening to the body.

- To be with people who are not supportive of your growth and expansion.

- To abuse substances such as alcohol, marijuana, cocaine, or prescription medicine.

- To watch many hours of television or spend many hours surfing the Internet or playing video games.

- To be addicted to Internet pornography.

- To isolate yourself.

Changing Negative and Self-Destructive Thinking

Changing behavior, habits, and our ability to make healthy decisions is not a simple thing.

Our behavior and habits are based on deep programming from our shame.

And when there is a lot of shame inside, we are very often trying to soothe ourselves with cigarettes, alcohol, or TV.

Perhaps we do not choose the best or the healthiest way to meet that need, but it is still important to validate our decisions, habits, and actions from the loving space of understanding the need we are trying to meet, and the thoughts that stimulate it rather than judge it.

There are basically two ways to change negative and self-destructive thinking, behavior, and habits: either *"bottom/up"* or *"top/down"* *change.*

Top/down change means that we can use our clarity and discipline to alter our behavior, decisions, or habits once we become aware of the price we are paying for doing it and the benefits we would gain from changing it. We call it. "top/down" because it is using our discipline and cognition to exact change.

The top/down approach involves:

- Introducing new healthy habits and routines into our lives, such as starting to move the body regularly and eat healthier.

- Being more aware of important decisions that we are making in our life—such as in relationships and in work situations—to see if they are in tune with or violate our being.

- Taking some small risks to confront fears and insecurities.

This approach is extremely helpful.

But it alone is not enough.

Our actions, decisions, and habits also change when we take the healing journey that we have described in this handbook.

We don't actually *do it*, it *happens*.

We call this *"bottom/up change."*

It happens indirectly as a result of working with our wound of shame.

Here is an example:

Elaine spent twenty-five years married to Tony and raised their three children mostly alone because Tony, a wealthy businessman, was seldom at home. He cheated on her regularly, but she had no idea he was being unfaithful. When she discovered the truth, she entered into a lengthy and painful divorce process. For six years afterward, she dated men casually but was too shamed and afraid to become serious with any other man. She applied herself to individual and group therapy, unraveled her profound shame about herself as a woman, and was able to admit to herself that she never felt worthy of being with a man who truly loved her. However, one year ago, something changed. She fell deeply in love with a man who cherishes her, who has all the qualities she has looked for in a man, and she feels that for the first time in her life, she knows what it is to love and be loved. She is not able to say what or how things changed, but she feels deeply different inside. She feels worthy to receive this affection.

Here is another example for how the bottom/up approach heals:

Betty has struggled since childhood with her weight. She would like to lose thirty-five pounds and has tried many different diets, but nothing worked. Even strict regimens of cutting out sugar and carbohydrates only helped her lose a few kilos for a while, but then she gained the extra weight back very quickly. She also found that this "top/down" approach made her constantly obsessed with food and her weight. Then she dove into the "bottom/up" approach of working deeply with her shame and her negative body image, and she discovered that her problem with food had developed as a way of soothing herself from her traumatic childhood with an absent mother and a violent father. In the past two years, she has been slowly dropping the weight with only minor discipline in her eating habits.

The way we can inspire and encourage bottom/up change is by putting our totality, commitment, and energy into doing the inner work for healing shame as Elaine and Betty did.

The results will begin to show themselves in our lives gradually but convincingly with time.

However, we cannot predict or expect results according to a timetable or an agenda.

Change happens mysteriously and often when we least expect it.

However, the bottom/up approach of working deeply on our wounds is often not enough.

For instance, Mark has struggled with trying to stop smoking cigarettes for a long time. He has done deep and consistent therapy on all the emotional issues surrounding his smoking addiction but it has not enabled him to stop. Once, some years ago, he managed to quit for six months but started again when he had a cigarette at a party after drinking quite a bit of alcohol. Once having started, he could no longer smoke casually. Mark will need to apply the top/down approach of abstention if he wants to quit for good.

We can definitely support our growth process by combining both approaches.

Timothy is working regularly with weekly therapy sessions and periodic seminars with us. At our suggestion, he has also begun a regular daily exercise routine of either running, swimming, or spinning. He says that after his workout, he has a "four-hour high." He feels better about himself because he is bringing some discipline to his life, he feels more energy in his body, and also notes that as a result of his exercising, he now has much more space and ability to observe and feel his wounded self in different situations in his life. In addition, he is taking risks by spending more time alone rather than automatically going out to drink and socialize with his friends.

Too much discipline, risk, and regimentation can easily make us rigid and dry. Also, too much discipline can lead to failure and even more shame and discouragement.

But without some discipline, we can easily remain stuck in our old shame thinking and habits. Too little discipline can prevent us from making progress because we can rehash the shame thoughts, behaviors, and feelings over and over again without taking the risk to come out of our comfort zone.

We encourage small steps and building on small but progressive successes.

We experience over and over again in our work that combining both approaches is the best way to bring significant and lasting change in your life.

Exercise 1:

1. Pick an area of your life in which you feel successful or fulfilled.

2. Notice how you think about yourself and life when you put your focus on this area. Write your thoughts down.

3. Now, pick an area of your life in which you feel inadequate and unfulfilled.

4. Notice how you think about yourself and life when you focus on this area of your life. Write your thoughts down.

Exercise 2:

Examine some major decisions and habits you have made or still make in your life.

1. Can you sense which ones were shame-based decisions?

2. Can you sense what motivated you to make these decisions and what needs you might have been trying to meet?

3. Can you sense which of your habits are shame-based?

4. Can you sense what need you were/are trying to meet with these habits?

5. Have you noticed that any of these habits, behaviors, or decisions has changed as a result of doing inner work on your shame?

As you examine any habits that you feel are negative, is there some *small* change that you could make to help you feel better about yourself in this area?

If so, what would it be and how would it make you feel?

Is there any kind of small risk you could take that would give you greater self-esteem and a sense of more mastery of your life?

CHAPTER 13:

HEALTHY SHAME

Our discussion of shame would not be complete unless we also mention what is called, *"healthy shame."*

Once we begin to recover from what we have been discussing so far that has been called "toxic shame," we are also much more able to allow ourselves to feel and learn from the appropriate experience of shame.

This is the shame we feel when we have done something that was hurtful to someone.

It is the shame we might feel when we have performed something but inside we know that we were not as total or as responsible as we could have been.

Finally, it is the shame we might feel when we are not living our truth, a topic that we will take up in more detail in the next volume of the Learning Love Handbook.

Shame in its essence is not actually a negative emotion because when experienced appropriately, it is like a beacon in the dark guiding us to live with more heart, dignity, and purpose.

Unfortunately, the way most of us were raised, shame is taken over by our harsh and punitive inner critic and buries our intuition, life energy, courage, spontaneity, and optimism.

Healthy shame is a "wake-up call." It is an inner loving guide telling us to feel the pain and apologize if we have hurt someone, to apply ourselves more totally if we have done something in a shoddy way, or to listen to our potential and take action. It reminds us to take risks, live our destiny, and keep growing spiritually and emotionally.

That is quite different from "toxic shame."

As we are talking about healthy vs. toxic shame, we also need to mention the difference between what we call, "supportive and condemning guilt."

Supportive guilt comes together with healthy shame when we have done something that was hurtful to another or to ourselves, when we are delaying to develop, explore, and express our gifts, or if we are engaging in an activity that is clearly self-destructive.

Condemning guilt is the guilt we feel when:

- We have done something and we are afraid of what others might think.

- We do something that goes against our inner critic or our family tradition.

A big part of our healing from shame is learning to distinguish between these two kinds of shame and guilt. In that way our inner wisdom can help guide us to discover greater dignity and self-worth as opposed to living with the burden of toxic shame and condemning guilt that only deepens our lack of self-love.

CONCLUSION:

In the first part of this handbook, we have outlined a journey of healing shame.

In life this can be one of the most challenging struggles that anyone of us will have to go through.

Shame is a powerful force that can cripple us with depression, self-judgments, negativity, sickness, and even loss of the desire to live.

When we are taken over by shame, we can lose the hope of ever having love in our lives.

We may no longer believe in love and can become bitter and cynical. Our shame tells us that we don't deserve to be loved and happy.

It can make us lose hope that we will ever find our creativity and contribute in a way that feels deeply nourishing.

Yet, it is possible to recover from this wound.

We end by providing some simple suggestions that might help you on your journey:

1. Recognize that insecurity, self-doubt, and shame *happened to you; you were not born with it.*

2. Know that *everyone makes mistakes*—that is *how you learn.*

3. Be aware that the *inner judge is not telling you the truth* because whatever does not come with an energy of love cannot be true.

4. Slowly learn to *observe your body, thoughts, and behavior without judging,* but just as an impartial, loving witness.

5. *Discover and develop the unique gifts* that you have to offer in this life and know that it is your mission to discover and express them.

6. Introduce *positive habits* into your life such as exercising regularly, eating a healthy diet, engaging in a simple and short meditation practice, spending time in nature, and being with loving friends who can help you recover your self-love.

PART 2

UNDERSTANDING AND HEALING
FEAR AND SHOCK

CHAPTER 1:

A SIX-STEP APPROACH TO WORKING WITH OUR FEARS

I n this part of the handbook, we would like to present a simple method for dealing with our fears that has proved to be effective in our lives and the lives of those we work with.

Fear is perhaps the most significant issue that all of us have to deal with in our lives. For us in our work and in our lives, we have found that coming to terms with fear is the basis of a fulfilling life. But we need a simple and practical way to understand and work with it.

We have attempted to reduce the work involved in managing fear to six simple steps. They are not linear, but together, they make up what we feel is a comprehensive approach. We will be discussing each step in some detail, but here is an outline of this six-step method that we would like to guide you through:

1. The first step deals with *becoming aware of how we avoid acknowledging and feeling our fears*. It concerns all the ways that we compensate and distract ourselves from fear with behaviors such as

pushing, isolating, selling ourselves, bragging, aggressing, rescuing, complaining, and all kinds of addictions.

2. The second is learning to *recognize when we are in fear* and to become conscious of all the ways that it *shows* itself. This includes tuning into the *body sensations* of fear. It includes observing what we call *fear-driven thinking*. And finally, it includes becoming conscious of our *fear-driven behaviors*. In this step, we begin to observe these three areas—sensations in the body, fear thinking, and fear behavior as they show up in our daily lives.

3. The third involves *getting to know our trauma story*. This step concerns learning how we experienced fear as children in situations in which we were abandoned, disrespected, exposed to aggressive environments, and in general felt helpless and threatened. Learning our fear story is not an intellectual exercise; it is feeling our story from the inner perspective of an innocent and trusting child.

3. The fourth concerns noticing *what triggers our fear* in our lives today. In this step, we begin to notice what we call "our sensitivities"— the situations and environments, as well as our own thoughts and behaviors or behaviors of others—that provoke a fear response in us.

5. The fifth step of this approach to managing fear deals with learning *how to be with fear* when it arises in our lives and how to soothe ourselves by relaxing our nervous systems. Specifically, this includes paying close attention to the sensations of fear by embracing them with a quality of loving presence much like a mother or father holding a frightened child. It also includes practicing breathing exercises that we will discuss and finding activities that relax us other than using addictive substances.

6. And finally, the sixth step of our method concerns *taking action*. Taking action means introducing small risks in our lives to challenge and overcome deeply ingrained fear patterns. It includes learning to

stand up for ourselves by setting limits when appropriate. It also includes strengthening our resources, moving our bodies with regular exercise, adopting healthy, vitalizing habits of eating well, and planning our days in constructive ways. Finally, taking action also includes introducing a dosage of discipline into our lives so that we don't allow the frightened younger part of us inside to dictate our behavior. This young part wants instant gratification, does not do well with tolerating frustration, and hates to feel fear. So taking action means ensuring that our wiser self is in charge of our life and not the wounded part of us. In that way we begin to live our life guided by our wisdom instead of directed by our fear.

Let's begin the journey.

CHAPTER 2:

HOW DO WE RELATE WITH OUR FEAR?

The approach to dealing with and healing fear and its frozen cousin, shock, that is detailed here has been partly inspired by the work of Peter Levine (called Somatic Experiencing), and we would like to express our gratitude and appreciation for his work and books. His method of working with fear by focusing on the body sensations is ground breaking because it directs the attention away from mind concepts to the nervous system, where the fear lives. (References to Peter's books are provided at the end of this handbook.)

Let's begin by looking more deeply at fear—why we have it, how we avoid it, what it feels like, how to deal with it, and the gifts that it brings us.

We all have fear.

We are vulnerable beings in this world, never knowing if we will be taken care of, or if we will be loved, harmed, judged, rejected, or betrayed.

And in an existential sense, we never know when sickness or even death will take us. When we live with awareness, we realize that we are ultimately vulnerable and the most significant events of our lives are not in our hands.

Each one of us may relate very differently to the fear that we have inside.

Some of us may do all we can to avoid feeling fear. We may even deny that we have fear and create our lives in such a way that we don't have to feel or face it.

We may judge fear in ourselves or in others, and when it comes up, we do whatever we can to push through it.

Some of us may avoid feeling fear by escaping into one of many forms of addictive behaviors such as drinking alcohol, using drugs, engaging in extreme sports, being obsessed with sexual experiences, watching television, or being addicted to the Internet.

Or we may retreat into pleasing others and doing everything we can to avoid conflict.

Some of us may be crippled by fear. It can be so strong that we may even shrink from life.

Our fears may hold us back from starting new things, from taking risks to express ourselves, from social situations, or from opening up to another person.

Our hidden fears can create deep mistrust of life, others, and ourselves.

One way or another, we all try to deal with the fear we have inside.

But in order to find peace with ourselves and with life, it is important to find a loving, gentle, and graceful way to embrace our fear, understanding where it comes from and how to deal with it when it comes up.

Undoubtedly we have had many experiences in our live that caused tremendous fear and damaged our trust.

In some cases, we may have buried the fear memories deep in our unconscious and cling to the idea that everything was fine when we were a child.

In other cases, we may be well aware of experiences that were fearful, but we choose to forget them and believe that because they are in the past, they can no longer affect us.

Actually, just the opposite is true!

Experiences of fear lie hidden in our body and in our mind and will deeply affect our lives and our ability to relate to others.

And when we don't become aware of these experiences and work through them, they can easily sabotage our lives.

They will show themselves as *body symptoms,* as *a tendency to avoid any situation that can bring up fear,* or they can cause us to lead a life of *falseness and compensation.*

The way for us to recover from fear begins with us acknowledging the depth of our fear.

There may be many moments when our fear arises in our daily lives:

- We are about to have an important meeting and we are afraid of the outcome.

- We need to make a presentation and we are afraid that we might not do a good job.

- We are going to a party and we are afraid that we will not make a good impression or will not know what to do and how to relate.

- We are meeting someone we are attracted to and may be afraid he or she will not like us or find us attractive.

- We are making love and afraid that we will not be a good enough lover.

- We need to take an important exam or compete in a sport and are afraid that we will fail or lose.

- We are afraid to come close to someone because he or she might judge, reject, disrespect, or overpower us.

- We are in deep connection with someone and may be afraid to lose that person.

- We may be afraid of not having enough money to live comfortably.

- We may be afraid of getting ill or have constant worries at night about uncertain aspects of our lives.

- We may be afraid to express our truth to someone, and hide instead.

Some of us have constant fear, and we don't even know why.

For instance, Mario, a forty-five-year-old Italian man, is timid and held back in her energy. He talks hesitantly and is fearful of change or any kind of new experiences or adventures. In his relationship with Tina, his wife, he allows himself to be controlled and micromanaged because he is too scared to stand up to her in any way. But he is not aware that he is carrying a great deal of fear because he has lived in this way as long as he can remember.

Our fear may show itself as panic, a chronic sense of restlessness, a racing heartbeat, sweating, feeling dizzy, nauseous, weak, or shaky on our feet, or we may notice that much of the time, we are not really there and feel frozen and confused.

In the following chapters, we will take you step by step to explore different aspects of fear and shock and look at how you can find a gentle way to be with fear when it comes up.

Our journey through fear is one of the deepest and most significant explorations that we can do because fear is such a dominant force in life.

Until we learn to deal with our fear, it can easily run our lives by determining our behavior, our attitude toward life, and our sense of ourselves.

But once we learn to understand, develop profound compassion for ourselves when we have fear, and learn the tools to transform and feel fear, it actually becomes a source of strength, depth, and aliveness.

CHAPTER 3:

HOW DOES FEAR SHOW ITSELF?

There are many ways that fear can show itself, and it is important to learn to recognize these signs of fear.

One sign we call "*active fear*," and it happens when our nervous system speeds up and is in overdrive.

In this kind of fear, we become agitated; everything may seem to be going very quickly. We talk, eat, move, think, and react quickly. We may be on super-alert, as Alexandra is.

Alexandra experiences fear with very slight provocations. Her legs begin to shake, and she feels so anxious that she has to get away from wherever she is as fast as possible. "I am not sure what triggers my shaking and anxiety, but I know that it happens anytime I get angry, if someone yells or screams at me or even comes near me, or if I feel pressured in any way." She cannot say when this reaction started because she has few clear childhood memories. She is aware that it has gotten worse lately but does not know why.

Another way that fear can show itself is with what is called *shock* or "*frozen fear*."

Shock is a state in which many of our normal nervous system functions simply don't work properly.

When we are in shock, we may find it difficult to think clearly, to move, to talk, or even to feel anything. We may feel emotionally numb.

We may no longer be able to do something that we normally could do easily and without effort.

When we are in shock, we may faint, have accidents, become forgetful or confused, or our minds may become blank.

Or on an even deeper level, shock may show itself as body symptoms such as skin problems, chronic irritation of the bowel, cold hands and feet, chronic back pain, stuttering, forgetfulness, being prone to accidents, difficulty concentrating or retaining information, or inability to listen when someone is teaching or talking.

It was a huge revelation when Thomas, a thirty-four-year-old doctor from Germany, realized that he had been in shock much of his life. He began to recognize that his coming prematurely in sex was because he put so much pressure on himself to be a good lover and because deep inside, he was very afraid of women. He realized that often when he had to speak in public, take a test, or compete in a sport, he went into shock, and this affected his performance. He realized that many times he had trouble breathing and felt tight in his chest, but often he had no idea why. Now he knows that it is fear. He also realized that he was much more afraid of becoming close to a woman than he had ever suspected. He saw that his shyness as a child was because he had been in shock much of the time. It was such a relief to understand that his period of bedwetting as a child had stemmed from fear and that the fear had begun when his parents divorced when he was six years old.

In short, when we are in fear, our nervous systems can either slow down or speed up.

Our fear may be *acute,* such as when an attack of panic or anxiety is provoked by some event or thought, or we may be in a *chronic* state of anxiety that seems to underlie our daily lives, particularly after we have experienced a painful failure or rejection.

We may not be able to rest or sleep, or we may feel tired and sleepy all the time. We may have diarrhea or constipation. We may feel chronically excited with high energy, or tired and phlegmatic with low energy. We may push until we burn out or collapse, or we may shrink our life energy.

Fear also causes a *tightening in our muscles.*

We may have a permanent tightening of our muscles because of chronic fear or tightening only whenever we feel unsafe and threatened.

When we are afraid, our breathing gets shallow or we feel that we can't get a deep full breath?

That is because the muscles of our chest have tightened in fear. The more we get stressed, the harder it is to breathe.

Or we may feel pain in our back from chronic stress and tightening of our back and neck muscles because of fear.

Another common sign of fear and shock is *spacing out or dissociating.*

Have you noticed that sometimes when someone is talking, you don't hear him or her?

Or that you are doing something and you don't feel like you are really there?

Or maybe you notice that you were someplace, but you can't remember anything about the experience.

In these times, you were probably dissociated.

Finally, another sign of fear, one that might be hard to recognize, is *anger and irritability.*

When our fear is provoked, it can cause us to feel helpless and remind us of earlier times when we were helpless. And that feeling of helplessness causes us to get angry or irritable because it provokes so much fear of unknown and potentially dangerous or painful consequences.

When we feel helpless, we are vulnerable to being invaded, abused, humiliated, or neglected.

Normally, we all want to feel a sense of mastery over life and a sense that we can manage and deal with any situation that arises.

Helplessness is the opposite feeling, and most often we don't like it!

Now, whenever we feel out of control and our helplessness gets provoked, we may easily feel irritated and angry and blame someone or something. This is the predicament that Richard often finds himself in:

Richard routinely gets angry whenever he gets upset and stressed. Then he blames and strikes out at his wife. In these moments he actually believes that he is justified in his anger explosions and blaming. He somehow finds some reason to find fault in her—either she was too messy, chaotic, noisy, bossy, or not present enough. Sometimes, when there is no one around to get angry at, he rages at life, or when driving, he rages at other drivers for the way they drive. Then he yells in his car in the hope of blowing off some steam. None of these strategies really work. When he blames and accuses his wife, he feels guilty later, and when he has road rage, he sees how ridiculous he is being. But neither guilt nor remorse gets to the root of the problem. His nervous system is like a tight spring holding all his fear and tension inside. He would rather rage than feel and be with his fear and helplessness because that has always been his habit.

The feeling of helplessness can also cause depression. It is another reaction to the intolerable sense that you cannot control our life and our destiny.

In order to avoid feeling helpless, we may have eating disorders or weight problems, or experience chronic fatigue.

Exercise:

Take a moment to see if any of the symptoms we have described above relate to your life:

1. Do you sometimes have trouble with your digestion—either diarrhea or constipation—and is the problem related to greater stress?

2. Do you have sexual difficulties such as premature ejaculation, difficulty getting or keeping an erection, or an inability to have orgasms or feel your body or your sexual energy? Might this be related to feeling unsafe, or to some kind of pressure or fear?

3. Do you sometimes have difficulty breathing or tightness in your chest and is this related to stressful situations?

4. Do you find that sometimes you have difficulties with remembering things, absorbing information, losing things, thinking clearly, expressing yourself, feeling emotions, or feeling paralyzed? Could these symptoms be related to feeling pressure, expectations, anger from someone, or feeling insecure?

5. Do you sometimes have episodes of trembling, shaking, sweating, or having cold extremities? Can you sense what may be provoking these episodes?

CHAPTER 4:

HOW DOES FEAR AFFECT OUR LIVES?

Fear has a profound influence on our lives, and unless we become aware of it and take a journey to learn how to be with our fear, it will have many negative effects on us.

It can sabotage our intimate relationships, our creativity, our sexuality, our health, and our general attitudes toward life, others, and ourselves.

This sabotage happens because we unconsciously react from fear when we want to avoid feeling it.

As we have mentioned earlier, behind our fear is a deep feeling of helplessness.

When we don't take time to feel the fear and helplessness, we usually react in very common ways.

Let's explore some of the main ways that we might do this.

Reacting with Aggression

One way is to become *aggressive.*

We may deal with any sense of helplessness and fear by pushing, trying harder, and by being competitive, tyrannical, and insistent on having things go our way and being right.

This attitude toward fear is to deny that it is there or to push through it at all costs. With this attitude, we may believe that if we paid any attention to the fear, it would take over, and we wouldn't be able to function.

This approach makes it difficult for people to feel safe and be open with us.

And when we push ourselves so hard, we may want to soothe the constant stress with some form of substance such as alcohol, cocaine, or other drugs.

Or we may become addicted to sex or pornography or some other activity.

Michael's story illustrates what can happen when we constantly deny our fears:

Michael is a successful and wealthy businessman who has been pushing himself all his life. In addition to being hard working, he is also a marathon runner, thin and fit, and used to solving any problem that he has had to face in his life. Unfortunately, his relationship with his wife and two children has not gone well. His wife left two years ago because she could no longer stand the lack of communication and sensitivity from him. She had tried for years to get some kind of connection with him, but finally gave up. Michael's children are estranged from him because they both feel that they cannot reach him, and feel judged, pressured, and unseen by him. It is the failure of these relationships that finally drove him to therapy. However, he still cannot accept our suggestion that he has deep fears inside that he has not touched.

Fear, he claims, is what holds people back. He claims that he has been successful in life because he pushes through any fears that come up.

Michael's rigid, determined, hard, fixed beliefs and ways of approaching life cause people around him to be afraid and compliant. They cannot truly open up to him because he shows no vulnerability and no opening for someone to come in. Others may be pleasing and compliant toward Michael, but inside, they feel afraid and resentful. The way he judges and pressures others is the same way he treats his own frightened inner self. And because he is so disconnected from his fearful side, he creates relationships with lovers and his children that reflect this part of him that he rejects. The frightened part of him is his disowned self, and others are mirroring it for him.

Michael's style of behaving toward fear is by no means limited to men. Harriet, for example, is a highly successful businesswoman. Her father is a billionaire entrepreneur, and her goal as a child was to earn his respect. Instead of going to work for him, she created her own business that became so successful that a multinational company wanted to buy her out for a fortune. But she refused because she wants to remain outside of the influence of her powerful father. Unfortunately, however, her business acumen does not extend to her relating skills. Her husband has become increasing frustrated at her inability to be vulnerable and her refusal to make time to explore why their relationship is not working.

Reacting with Submissiveness

Another common reaction to the feeling of helplessness is to become *submissive or pleasing*.

We may have developed this strategy to keep harmony and to not present any kind of threat or confrontation so no one will hurt us.

We may believe that as long as we give in, comply, and surrender our own needs and desires, we will be treated kindly.

Also, we may believe that by being submissive, we will get the love and appreciation that we so long for. And we may even create a spiritual ego that feels that by being submissive, we are a "kind, good, and holy person."

The price we pay with this approach is to become a victim, to lose our dignity and self-respect, to invite other people to take advantage of us, and eventually to run the risk of becoming bitter, resentful, and angry inside because we are abandoning our own needs.

Suzanne, for example, is married to a successful surgeon, has three teenage children, and lives in a spacious home in the suburbs. Her husband is sexually demanding and sometimes rages at her when things in the home are not as he wants. She feels helpless and dependent but realizes that she has behaved this way with every man she has been with in her life. She does not know or feel what she needs, so it is automatic for her to comply with whatever the man wants and needs. Inside, she has lost love and respect for herself. Furthermore, she has structured her life in such a way that security and comfort are guaranteed. Her parents are proud that she is in such a comfortable marriage and that she has no worries for her financial needs. But she is no longer attracted to her husband, she finds herself bored and depressed, and her oldest child has become involved with drugs and alcohol. She feels no real joy in her life.

Reacting by Withdrawing from Life

Another strategy for avoiding feeling the helplessness and fear is to *withdraw from life* and limit our experiences so that we don't run the risk of being hurt or rejected.

This can also take the form of living in a fantasy world or of being mystified and giving our power and responsibility away to spiritual teachers or to a religion. The story of Alicia demonstrates what can happen when we withdraw into a fantasy world:

Alicia, a forty-five-year-old woman, reads romance novels and imagines that someday she will finally find a man who will truly love, protect, and take care of her. She deals with the rejections she has received in the past from men with spiritual platitudes such as, "it is all for the good; God is directing my life, and all I have to do is keep trusting in God." She traveled all the way to India to visit a guru who, she had heard, magically removes "bad karma," but she came back disappointed. She regularly pays "healers" to fix her but has still not found the right one who can solve her problems. She has the belief that if she pretends to be joyful and only says positive things, this will change her. Still, she remains lonely and sad. She does not believe in therapy because, she says, it only brings up "bad thoughts." When Alicia talks, she has a dreamy quality and seems removed from what she is talking about and from the other people in the seminar. To come out of her fantasy world and become present to reality, she would have to face all the fears that she has avoided. But she is terrified. Alicia's fantasies and her hopes that she will find someone who will rescue her have created a safety zone for her, a way of being in a world that in her childhood was unkind and violent. Without creating these illusions and fantasy world, she might not have been able to survive the violence she experienced as a child

This strategy of withdrawal might also lead us to escape into drugs, alcohol, or food.

Deep inside, the wounded and frightened part of us may feel so overwhelmed and anxious that we feel compelled to soothe ourselves with some substance.

Alan is a good example of someone who practices this kind of avoidance. He has many girl friends at the same time, and even has a philosophy of "polyamory" (having several lovers at the same time) to justify his sexual addiction. He enjoys extreme sports such as mountain climbing and paragliding and frequently does cocaine. He loves his freedom. Only recently has he questioned his lifestyle because he fell in love with a woman who left him after a year when he told her that he had made love to another woman. She insisted that it was impossible to come close to him. Underneath Alan's freedom-seeking lifestyle, there are many hidden fears—the fear of being rejected, exposed, hurt, or becoming dependent on someone.

Only a strong motivation to change, a topic we will discuss in the next chapter, would inspire someone with this kind of lifestyle or habits to explore the deeper fears inside.

Reacting by Rescuing Others

A fourth common way of avoiding feeling our helplessness is by *rescuing others*.

If we can distract ourselves by saving another person from his or her fear, we don't have to feel our own.

There is also some ego gratification from being a rescuer because it allows us to feel useful and needed.

But the price we pay is that we can burn out and get resentful that others are not giving back to us.

Underneath our giving is almost always a hidden desire to receive, but we might be reluctant to feel or admit that we are afraid, needy, and vulnerable

Andre is a fifty-nine-year-old man who became wealthy as a real estate developer. He is caring and supportive of his employees and other people whom he feels are in need. In his relationships with women, including his current relationship, he provides financially. He gains a lot of gratification from this behavior and even describes himself as "a generous and caring man." But his wife complains that he is not really open or available and uses his care-taking as a way of staying in power and control. While she appreciates his generosity, she is also furious about how he controls her and needs to have his way.

Keeping Our Lives Busy and Chaotic

Finally, another common way that we may avoid feeling fear is by living our lives with constant activity, staying preoccupied with planning, appointments, projects, or distractions, and creating an aura of chaos around us.

For example, Alison is a highly intelligent, attractive, charming, and skilled body oriented therapist. She is also a single mother of a ten-year-old son. She fills her life with so many activities, responsibilities, and people who rely on her for support that she leaves no time for herself. She talks and moves very fast, is commonly late for appointments because she attempts to juggle so much at once, and her home looks like it was hit by a hurricane. In her relationships with men, she always puts their needs above her own until she reaches a point that she feels so tired of being there for them that she explodes. Her continual activity and chaos covers a deep fear that she would never be loved she allowed herself to express what she needs.

Why These Approaches Are Not the Solution

These approaches to avoiding feeling the helplessness may work on the surface and may give us an identity and a strategy for dealing with life and with our fear. But they also keep us disconnected from ourselves and from our vulnerability.

Sometimes, when we have disconnected from our fears in such a radical way, they will show themselves with pains or illnesses in the body, or we may have a serious accident.

Or they show themselves when a part of our lives falls apart, especially in significant relationships.

However, and this is an important point, as we take the journey of exploring and connecting with our fears and helplessness, *we also have to take into consideration our needs for safety and security.*

When we have fear hidden in our unconscious, we may be very afraid of feeling and connecting with the fear because we believe that it will overwhelm us and take over.

So this journey of uncovering and feeling fear takes time, patience, and perseverance.

Exercise:

Take a moment to consider your life and see if you can recognize how you might be avoiding feeling helplessness and fear.

For each of the following behaviors, ask yourself how this behavior helps you deal with feelings of helplessness:

1. Do you see yourself using any of the following behaviors as a way of not feeling: television, shopping, excess sugar consumption, sex, drugs, alcohol, or work?

2. Do you find yourself frequently getting angry or irritable when you are anxious or stressed?

3. Do you become aggressive and project that aggression onto others? Or do you judge, criticize, and pressure other people for being afraid and collapsed?

4. Do you structure your life in such a way as to avoid risk and fearful situations?

5. Do you approach life in a magical way hoping to be rescued, taken care of, protected, or loved unconditionally?

6. Do you often space out in situations that might feel threatening to you?

7. Do you play the role of the rescuer?

8. Do you put other people's needs before your own needs?

9. Do you push your body and not listen to what it needs?

CHAPTER 5:

WHY DO WE HAVE SO MUCH FEAR?

Paolo's father was a rage-aholic. His outbursts were violent and unpredictable, and he often beat Paolo when he did not behave the way that his father expected. Paolo, a sensitive and refined artist, dealt with this abuse by retreating into himself and trying to get away from his father's toxic energy in any way he could. His mother was absent from the home much of the time, didn't protect him from his father's behavior, and wasn't able to stand up for herself. She told Paolo that "this is just the way your father is and you have to get used to it." Paolo could never stand up to his father even as he got older, and his father died without the abuse ever being mentioned. Now, Pablo suffers from crippling depression. He has not yet felt or come to terms with the powerful helplessness that his father's treatment and his mother's neglect caused in him.

Some of the fear we feel today is existential.

We are vulnerable to misfortunate, loss, illness, and death.

But an important source of the fear we experience today is a direct result to the traumas we experienced as a child. These traumas have significant residual effect on our thinking, body experience, and behavior today.

An important part of our journey of healing from fear is knowing where our trauma comes from and having deep compassion for the little boy or girl inside of us that still holds this fear because of what happened to us.

When our trauma happened, a long time ago, we could not respond in an effective way to reduce or deal with the threat.

We were helpless.

We were too young to be able to confront the threat or go away from it. These are the two mechanisms that are built into our nervous systems to deal with threat. Without the ability to deal with it either through fight or flight, we chose the last option—that is, to play dead.

We froze and dissociated.

But when we are forced to choose freezing as a way of dealing with threat, the impact of the trauma stays in our bodies and we lose our aliveness and joy.

Instead of reducing the stress and bringing our nervous systems back to a relaxed state, we simply remained activated and aroused. In other words, our stress kept building up.

Let's take a look at the different ways we may have experienced trauma as a child:

1. *Invasion* (harshness, criticalness, rigidity, any kind of violence, anger, judgments, humiliation, pressure, unreasonable expectations, insensitivity, or bullying and teasing). Invasion also includes any kind of sexual invasion or disrespect of our sexual boundaries.

2. *Neglect* (lack of presence - parents who are not there for us physically, emotionally and energetically, lack of care, depression, substance abuse, being left or ignored by one or both parents, being sent away, or not being listened to or taken in).

3. *Environmental Trauma* (lack of care and hygiene in the home environment, insufficient money for food and clothing, frequent relocations to a new environment or school, hostility and anger in the home or a school). Can be caused by being brought up in a war zone, or any kind of natural disaster, such as an earthquake, hurricane, or tsunami.

4. *Hospitalizations and Medical Procedures* (injections, operations, being left alone in a hospital, or illnesses—especially chronic ones).

5. *Accidents* (any loss of control or physical injury can be devastating to a child).

As a child, we had little or no protection.

We experienced any kind of negative energy *in the environment* when we were a child as a direct assault on our nervous system, well being, and trust in the goodness of the world.

Negative energy or invasion can come in the form of physical, emotional, or sexual aggression and disrespect.

It can come as comparison, pressure, expectations, and repression of our natural life energy, as well as criticism, humiliation, mixed messages, neglect, or outright abandonment.

Any and all of these experiences will seem like a devastating trauma to a child.

And none of these trauma causes have to be extreme to cause tremendous fear.

It can be even worse for a child if the traumatic event is seemingly small but frequent and repetitive.

As a child, we didn't have the strength or resources to deal with or integrate these traumas.

We couldn't shake them off.

We couldn't go away, and we couldn't confront a big person who was disrespecting us.

We couldn't tell our parents to grow up or go into therapy.

Our attempts to get them to stop by abusing alcohol or drugs were usually not successful.

We couldn't bring a parent out of depression and make him or her happy, even if we tried.

We couldn't stop our father or mother from being angry.

We couldn't create a safe home environment.

As a child, we were helpless and at the mercy of the "big people."

The result is that we became traumatized and felt deeply helpless inside.

It is important to know *our trauma story*—more specifically, in what way neglect or invasion may have caused deep fear inside.

The specific events that happened to us create our sensitivities in our lives today.

Our sensitivities are the things that will trigger our fear and shock today—a topic we take up in the next chapter.

Exercise:

Take some moments to imagine yourself back as a small child in your home and school environment. It is a time when you are very young and full of innocence, curiosity, and trust.

Notice as you look out from the eyes and feel with the sensitivity of this little girl or boy:

- What does this environment(s) feel like? Is it safe or scary?

- What does this child need that he or she is not getting? In terms of safety, protection, security, warmth, affection, appreciation, and feeling wanted?

- What kind of energy is coming to him or her that might be frightening?

- Does he or she have someone to talk to who listens, or is he or she very alone?

As you reflect on these questions, you may begin to feel and understand how deeply you were traumatized as a child.

CHAPTER 6:

WHAT IS THE REASON TO RECONNECT WITH OUR FEAR?

You might ask, "What is the purpose of encountering and reconnecting with our fear and shock?

Clearly, there are advantages to keep denying it.

- We might be able to continue living as if it didn't exist.

- We might not have to face all the fears that we have repressed.

- If we stopped denying it, we might find that we are much more frightened than we could ever imagine.

But we would be missing something precious.

- When we deny our fear, it will not be safe for another person to open deeply to us. Our repressed fear will show itself as judgments, anger, irritability, criticism, or cynicism toward the other person or toward life. Most likely, we will be depriving ourselves of true love.

- When we deny our fear, we probably will seek to blame people and life when we get upset, and we could end up feeling bitter and frustrated.

- Denying our fear limits us and cuts us off from life and our true life energy. When we open ourselves to life, we open our deepest, most sensitive and vulnerable parts of us as well as the part of us that wants to live life fully.

- When we deny our fear, we can easily become hard, driven, compulsive, demanding, impatient, heartless, or addictive.

- When we deny our fears, they will show up in our bodies. Fears manifest themselves in the body, and if not owned, can tax our immune system, life energy, and motivation for life.

- When we are not in touch with our fear we push our bodies instead of listening to what it needs. With that pushing, we can easily burn out or eventually get depressed as we run out of energy.

It becomes quite convincing when we realize the price we pay for running from our fears and that can help motivate us to do the inner work for healing. As the stories of Tomas and Pietro highlight, even if we have been running from our fear for a long time, facing up to it can bring many benefits.

Tomas has always had the philosophy, something he learned from his father, that one should not pay any attention to fear. He never saw his father expressing or showing any kind of fear. Instead, his father was a man who pushed through any obstacle without complaining, was highly disciplined, worked hard, and seemed to enjoy his life in his stubborn and determined way. Tomas learned to be the same as his father and was disconnected from his fears and from all his feelings in much the same way his father was. Tomas never considered this a problem until he began to notice that it was having an effect on his intimate relationships. His lovers showed their fears openly and were sometimes overwhelmed and even crippled with fear and insecurity. For a long time, he felt that they were indulging their fears, and he would judge them for being collapsed. They complained that they could not feel him, that he was like a stone, and eventually they left him. Tomas continued to blame the women for not "understanding him" until he finally realized that this was a pattern that kept repeating itself. He decided to enter therapy. Tomas has now begun to realize that the price he has been paying for not connecting with his fear is the destruction of his relationships.

Peter is dependent on pain medication and is convinced that he needs to take this medicine regularly because of the constant pains in his body. He has been to many doctors, and none of them can find any physical cause for his pain. He meets any suggestion that his psychosomatic symptoms are a cover for his fear with a strong defensive objection and the claim that no one understands what he is going through. His wife finally reached a point where she could no longer tolerate his denial and gave him an ultimatum. She told him that if he didn't stop taking this pain medication and face the fears he is covering up with his addiction, she would leave him. He entered therapy very reluctantly, but his wife was clear that unless he was committed and persevered with deep ongoing therapy, she would divorce him.

The therapist made a condition for their work together that Peter stop taking pain medication under the direction and care of a doctor. It was very difficult in the beginning for him to handle the fears that surfaced in his body. But in the way that we will describe later, the therapist helped him to be with the panic in his mind and the fear symptoms in the body. With time, these panic symptoms subsided, and he began to discover that he has been living in fear all his life and that he had inherited the fear from his mother, who lives in fear much of the time, and desperately tries to control her environment and everyone around her. As he went deeper into feeling his fears, he discovered the anger he had for his mother for infecting him with so much fear and for trying to control him and his aliveness. The little boy in Peter was holding on to his mother by keeping his life energy low so he could stay energetically connected to her and was very frightened of coming fully alive and separating from mother.

Chronic pain, fatigue, sickness, and depression are common signs of fears that have been repressed, disowned, and not worked with.

If they remain repressed, they can seriously damage our lives.

Another motivation to deal with our fear is that we have compromised our lives to such an extent that we no longer find joy, passion, or meaning.

This is the case for Anna Lisa, who has been in a twelve-year marriage but no longer feels either love or attraction to her husband. She hates her conventional, boring lifestyle of pleasing and taking care of the needs of everyone around her and denying her own. But at the same time, the thought of breaking out of her box brings up absolute terror—terror of not having enough money to provide for herself, and terror of being alone, of being judged as selfish, and of facing the disapproval of her parents. She is now torn between opening to life or staying safe and knows that to do the former she has to face the fears she has been repressing all her life. She has been avoiding her life and her life energy by hiding and avoiding experiences that could bring up fear. The force of her unlived passion for life is beginning to rise like a volcano inside, asking to be lived.

These examples are some of the reasons that we become motivated to do the inner fear work.

Exercise:

Look over the list of things you might miss by not dealing with your fear. See which ones apply to you.

- Are you missing love in your life because it has not been safe for someone to come close to you or because you have found excuses to avoid closeness?

- Do you routinely blame life or others when you are upset?

- Do you feel that you would like to be more alive; that you are missing something important in your life, and that you are compromising too much in your daily life?

- Do you find that you judge someone who is afraid or in shock?

- Are you impatient, driven, demanding, compulsive, and fanatical about your opinions?

- Do you sometimes have outbursts of rage that can easily be provoked or do you notice chronic irritability?

- Do you notice that you have unexplained pains in the body, fatigue, burn out, or digestive, nervous, skin, or sleeping problems?

CHAPTER 7:

WHAT ARE OUR SENSITIVITIES?

In a recent workshop we were leading, Susanna, a thirty-four-year-old woman from Switzerland, became extremely agitated by the loud music that we played during a dance structure. She began screaming and needed to leave the room before she could settle down. When she returned, she was quite angry with us for selecting that specific kind of music and felt that we had been insensitive to her. We asked her if loud music reminded her of something from her childhood. At first she just wanted to blame us for causing her distress, but after she had settled down she could see that the loud music reminded her of her chaotic home environment. Her father had often raged unpredictably at her and her mother and her mother had done nothing to protect her.

Our nervous system becomes chronically agitated when we cannot resolve the traumas of our past and we have absorbed the energy that was not loving or harmonious.

Today, because we already live with so much inner tension, the slightest trigger can cause agitation and bring on an attack of fear or put us into a state of shock.

Any trigger that even in the smallest way resembles something that caused our trauma in the past can do it.

Sometimes, just a smell, a picture, someone saying something, a certain situation, a look, a loud voice, or the slightest neglect can activate our fear and shock.

We call these small or large triggers *"our sensitivities."*

They are the events, inputs, and stimulations from the outside that cause us to re-experience the trauma that is in our bodies from past experiences.

When such an event happens, we have a spontaneous regression.

We are no longer here and now, but in a split second, without knowing it, we are there and then—back at the time when a trauma happened that left us feeling helpless and terrified.

Our particular sensitivities today are deeply related to what we experienced from the five sources of trauma that we mentioned earlier—invasion, (intrusion), neglect, environmental disharmony, accidents, or hospitalizations or medical procedures.

We can begin to discover our sensitivities by paying close attention to what triggers we today. Here are some possible situations that we may be sensitive to:

- A rejection, or just imagining that we have been rejected by someone we care about—for example, if someone is not listening to us, is not being totally present for us, is too busy, leaves the house, or spends too much time away.

- The fear of failure, of loud noises, or of someone giving us pressure, expectations, criticism, or judgments.

- When someone is angry with us or even when we sense someone's anger.

- Any kind of violence directed at us or at someone else.

- New environments or unfamiliar situations, or when we go traveling and leave the security of our home.

- The fear that we could hurt ourselves or that someone we love could hurt him- or herself or get sick.

- Starting something new or expressing ourselves in front of many people.

- Taking an exam, competing in sports, or being in a crowd or with new people.

It doesn't take much!

Exercise:

Take a moment to consider what situations in your life today trigger your fear or shock. Go over the list above and see if any of these could be one of your sensitivities.

CHAPTER 8:

OUR INNER SPLIT

Nicholas, a forty-two-year-old man from Germany, comes to a seminar with us for the first time. He has never done any kind of seminar before, but he is motivated because his relationship with his wife and children is not going well, he feels overburdened by all his responsibilities at work, he feels exhausted and burned out, and his health is suffering. As a child, he was conditioned to believe that success and productivity were what mattered. He learned to ignore any kind of fears and insecurity because he believed they would interfere with his ability to function effectively. He felt that he must keep his focus on the goal and discipline himself to do whatever it takes to accomplish these goals. As we began to help the participants to connect with the frightened part of them inside, he complained that he couldn't "feel anything." He wanted quick and practical solutions to the problems in his life and was frustrated that our approach did not offer these solutions fast enough.

Nicholas has an extreme split between two parts of him.

One part of him—and of all of us—is what we call *"the functional adult."*

This part of us values discipline, success, efficiency, productivity, results, aliveness, quick, practical solutions, and not getting distracted. It has no time or patience for failure, tardiness, self-indulgence, fear, insecurity, or shock.

Then there is the other part of him, also in all of us, *"the frightened and shocked child."*

This part of us lives with constant memories of invasions and neglect. It lives with memories of events from the past where we were helpless and terrified. It remembers experiences that occurred when we were small, when even the slightest lack of care or insensitivity—especially if these experiences were unpredictable and frequent—could bring the terror of not surviving. What this part of us longs for most of all is safety, security, softness, caring, and sensitivity. It lives in constant fear of whatever is unknown, unpredictable, unfamiliar, and uncertain.

When, as in Nicholas's case, we may have put all our focus, attention, and energy on the functional adult, we abandoned our frightened part and lost connection with it.

And most likely, we judged (and still judge) our own fear and insecurity and also the same qualities in others.

We can easily become impatient, judgmental, critical, hard, and demanding, and from that space, we can abuse others.

Nicholas shared with us later in the workshop that he had beaten his son in the same way that his father beat him. He believed it only helped his son to become stronger and couldn't understand the deep effect it had on his son's nervous system.

If we have a split between these two parts of us, the frightened child inside will hide, but show itself in indirect ways.

It might cause us to have accidents, to get sick, to become depressed, to burn out, or to sabotage our efforts at success.

In fact, when we have strongly disconnected from the frightened part of us, we can have extreme swings between high energy and collapse, between feeling alive and creative and suddenly depressed and without motivation. We may experience crippling back pain or sudden panic episodes. Or we may get moody and not know why or what happened to trigger our emotions.

In those moments, our frightened child has taken over.

Some of us have gone in the opposite direction from Nicholas. We have collapsed into our frightened children and abandoned our natural aliveness, energy, curiosity, enthusiasm, adventurous spirit, and joy.

For instance, Arun, a thirty-five-year-old man, experienced extreme pressure from his father to follow in his footsteps as a successful physician. Arun never had any interest in studying medicine but could not find his way in terms of a career. He spent some years involved in drugs, living in communities, and working at odd jobs to make a living. His father judged him as lazy and aimless and tried to motivate him by pushing him to find some kind of respectable work. This had the reverse effect on Arun, causing him to become depressed and listless. He continues to struggle with motivation and cannot overcome his dependency on marijuana.

The way to heal from this split between our functional adult part and our frightened, shocked part is to re-create a connection between these two parts of us.

Exercise:

There are a number of helpful ways that you can do this:

1. You can invite feedback from trusted friends as to how they experience this split between your functional adult and your frightened child.

2. You can begin to see your children (if you have children) as a mirror of your frightened child, especially in moments when they are frightened or insecure. (Children are generally much more deeply connected to their sensitivities and may not as yet have such a deep split between these two parts of themselves.)

3. You can begin to take time in a way that we will describe in a later chapter to observe and feel your frightened or shocked self.

4. You can begin to notice how you are judging other people for being weak, incompetent, too slow, or not motivated enough.

CHAPTER 9:

THE RED ZONE

Marco and Sandra are both artists working with glassblowing. They sell their beautiful products at art fairs in different cities. Whenever they have to get ready for a show, they have to load up their trailer carefully to protect the work, drive long distances, and finally set up their booth in the early morning to prepare for the fair. Both of them get very disturbed days before an art fair while frantically trying to get everything ready in time. They are short with each other, and every little upset can easily escalate into a vehement argument. Sometimes these fights get so intense that they both want to get a divorce. During the show, depending on how well they sell, they either stay disturbed or begin to relax. If they have had a successful show, they feel wonderful and return to being very loving with each other. They have come to recognize that their arguments have nothing to do with the relationship, and it has helped them immensely to realize that each of them simply becomes activated because of the stress and tension of preparing for and being in the art fair.

Imagine a barometer—a half circle with a needle in the middle.

The half circle is divided into three equal parts. On the left is what we call *"the relaxation zone,"* in the middle is *"the tension zone,"* and on the right is what we call *"the red zone"* or *"the overwhelm zone."*

Normally we live in the middle, *"the tension zone."*

This is what we call "baseline fear."

It is a level of fear that is almost always there, but because we have had this level of fear and tension for so long and perhaps become so accustomed to it, we may not perceive it as fear, but rather as a normal or familiar state. We have become used to it, adjusted to it, and learned to live with it.

We live in this state of low-grade tension for many reasons.

First, we all have a continual level of tension from early traumas that still affect our nervous system and have not been resolved.

Second, tension also comes from the ways that we judge, pressure, push, and criticize ourselves to be different. From all the ideals we have about how we should be.

It is this constant and often unconscious level of baseline fear and inner tension that takes a toll on our body in the form of chronic back pain, digestive disorders, skin conditions, ringing in the ears, and other chronic physical problems, some of which we talked about in previous chapters.

Our tendencies to drink alcohol, smoke cigarettes or marijuana, take medication, abuse sex, or distract ourselves in different ways are just symptoms of this chronic state of stress.

Sometimes, if we have had a good massage, taken a relaxing yoga class, spent some time in meditation, made beautiful, nourishing love, done some exhausting sports, gone to a spa, or taken a holiday, we may have a taste of *"the relaxation zone"*

We long to be in this zone.

We dream of being in a state of extended relaxation and inner peace.

We want to be free of stress, and much of our complaining comes from being in the tension zone and longing for the relaxation zone.

And our longing for this state is what attracts us to substances that can induce it temporarily.

It is a wonderful feeling, but it doesn't last if we are dependent on getting it from a substance, an activity, from sex, or even from another person.

We may have moments in the relaxation zone, but as soon as we are exposed to the stresses of everyday life—work and family responsibilities, or other concerns—we return to the tension zone.

Because we are in this constant inner tension, any stress from the outside, such as a big workload, a family conflict, a health concern, a loss, rejection, or failure, or a long wait in line or a traffic jam can easily move us into *"the red (or overwhelm) zone."*

When we are in the red zone, our nervous system goes into hyperactivity or shuts down and goes into shock. In other words, our inner tension shows itself as either active fear or frozen fear.

When we are activated in this way, we can easily become disturbed, reactive, emotional, impatient, judgmental, angry, or aggressive, or we shut down completely and dissociate.

When we are in the overwhelm zone, we want to get away.

And if we can't get away physically, we dissociate.

We may even want to strike out at someone because we feel so disturbed.

These are the times when we most want to soothe ourselves with some substance or distraction just to ease the tension.

Or we may create a fight because when we are in the red zone, we want to blame someone. This need to blame someone can be very compulsive.

Many of the problems that we face in our lives have less to do with the situations or people who have provoked us and much more to do with the fact that our nervous systems are disturbed, and we have entered into the red zone.

It is very helpful to know the state of our nervous system at any given moment.

We can observe the needle of our fear/tension barometer swinging from left to right depending on the circumstances around and inside us.

The more safe and familiar we feel in our environment, the less fear and tension.

The better and more confident we feel about ourselves, the less fear and tension.

When we have relaxed by being with a loved one, walking in nature, listening to quiet music, or being with an animal or perhaps a young child, we might notice our needle swinging to the left and entering the relaxation zone.

Exercise:

Begin to observe your level of fear and tension on a regular basis in everyday life.

- Notice what kinds of things cause the needle to swing to the right toward more tension, and even to the red or overwhelmed zone.

- Notice how you feel when you begin to enter the red zone. Feel the sensations in your body.

- Notice how you begin to react.

- Notice when situations or activities take you into the relaxation zone. How does it feel when you are in a still state?

CHAPTER 10:

LEARNING TO BE WITH OUR FEAR AND SHOCK

Anton, a forty-nine-year-old man, suffers from chronic anxiety. He has a high-powered job as a financial consultant and constantly stresses over the state of the economy and the welfare of his clients. When we talk to him, he speaks so quickly that it is hard to follow, and he seems always in a hurry.

When we invite him to notice what he is feeling in his body while he is talking, he says, "I can't feel anything."

We ask, "Do you notice any tightness in your chest, belly, or shoulders?"

"Well, now that you mention it, I do feel all of that. But they are always tight."

"What do you notice about your breathing?"

"My breathing is shallow."

"What else do you notice?"

"I feel anxious, like I always have to rush; I never have enough time. I can't catch my breath. And I feel butterflies in my stomach. I am afraid something bad is going to happen. That's why I talk and move fast. I can't slow down!"

"When you have that thought, how does that feel in your body?"

"Things just get worse. I can never relax except when I have a couple of drinks."

Anton has not taken the time to feel his body.

But when we call his attention to how he experiences the stress, he can see that his body shows it all the time.

In this chapter, we will be exploring the body sensations that fear and shock provoke and precisely how to cope with fear when it arises.

Active fear and frozen fear are different body experiences.

Hyperarousal that we feel when our active fear takes over causes a discharge of nervous energy that is easy to notice if you are paying attention to it and know what it is.

Sometimes the panic and hyperarousal sensations can be very extreme.

For instance, Laura has regular panic attacks for no apparent reason. She describes these episodes as devastating and terrifying. She says that she feels emptiness and darkness and a hollow feeling in her stomach. She begins to shake uncontrollably and is afraid that the fear will never end. In the past, she has taken medication for these attacks, but now she prefers to find a way to deal with the attacks without taking anything.

Many of us have panic symptoms that may not be as extreme as Laura but they are disturbing and confusing nonetheless.

Feeling frozen fear, or shock, is more challenging.

It is more difficult because shock is the absence of feeling, and the sensations that accompany shock are subtle.

When we are in shock, it may feel as if nothing is happening in the body, but actually there is always something happening; we just have to know how to become attuned to sensing it.

Simona, a thirty-eight-year-old woman, is in chronic shock, and appears to be removed and lacking energy. Her husband has rage attacks and frequently yells at her and the children. Her father had a similar tendency, and she became used to men being aggressive. For a long time, she has withstood her husband's abusive behavior without saying anything.

When we ask her how she feels when he is yelling, she says, "I have gotten used to it. He is stressed because of his work and is just letting off steam."

"Do you think that this behavior has an effect on you or the children?" we ask.

"Yes, sure it does. But it's just how it is."

"Let's imagine that your husband is right here and he is yelling. How do you feel in the body?"

"Actually, I never thought about it. But now that you mention it, I feel numb."

"Do you notice anything else?"

"I feel like I am not really here. It is as if I am watching a movie where someone is yelling and I am just watching from a distance."

"Was it the same when your father yelled?"

"Yes. That was how I dealt with it."

"Have you ever thought to say something to your husband when he is yelling?"

"Sure, I have! But in the moment, I can't find the words. And even if I know what I want to say before he starts yelling, when it is happening, I get totally confused."

"Do you have any emotions when he yells?" we ask.

"No, I don't have any feelings. It feels like all my feelings are turned off."

"Do you feel any anger when he yells at the children?"

"Yes, a little. But what's the point? He isn't going to change. Anyway, he is very stressed at work, so I have to accept it."

Simona's experience describes how many of us feel when we are in shock.

The sensations of tightness in the chest, shallow breathing, numbness, and feeling absent from the scene are almost universal, as is the inability to feel anything when we are being abused.

But it is not as though nothing is happening. If we pay close attention, we may be able to sense the numbness as a physical sensation. We may also notice in the moment when our shock is triggered that we have a tendency to space out and experience a sense of watching from a distance.

When we notice that we are experiencing fear and shock, no matter how strong the intensity, the most helpful way we have found to be with it is as follows:

1. Tell ourselves that we are in fear or shock. We call this *framing,* and it allows us to know that we are having a specific fear experience in the moment.

2. We can take a *few deep breaths* and perhaps place our hand on our heart just to settle ourselves a bit.

3. Now, we can take some moments to *track the fear or shock sensations in our body,* noticing how they affect our breathing, heart rate, muscle tension, dry mouth, and temperature or perspiration in our extremities. We

can perhaps notice numbness somewhere, lack of feeling, frozenness. Spacing out. A feeling of unreality.

4. We can notice any *thoughts* that come with the fear such as, "This will never go away, I am not going to make it," and so on. As we notice them, we can say to ourselves "These are just fear thoughts. I will choose not to pay attention to them."

5. If we are still feeling activated and agitated, we can *focus actively on our breathing*. We can practices some deep breathing exercises, as we will describe below.

6. We need to be patient; this process takes time.

Exercise:

The next time you experience fear or shock, follow the steps described above—frame your experience, take a few deep breaths, and then track the sensations in your body, notice fear thoughts, and focus on your breathing. Consider the fear as being like a wave and imagine that it is passing through.

You can also practice some breathing exercises as follows:

1. Take three deep breaths, slowly filling your lungs completely to the count of five and then exhale totally to the count of five. Place your hand on your heart to help take the energy away from your head and down to your body.

2. If the fear is quite intense, you can actually take fifteen deep breaths. This will help cool your nervous system and change your inner state.

3. Finally, you can do the same breathing exercise alternating nostrils. Inhale through the right to the count of five while closing the left; hold for five seconds, and then exhale through the left nostril, closing the right. Repeat. (This is a technique used in yoga practice.)

Guided Meditation on Fear and Shock Awareness

(You may wish to do this meditation by having a close friend or lover read it to you while you relax, lying or sitting in a comfortable and quiet place where you are not likely to be disturbed.)

Take some moments to relax your body.

Observe your breathing, and with each breath, allow yourself to go deeper and deeper inside.

Do this slowly, gently, taking your time.

There is no hurry. Just relax.

During this guided meditation, we will gently guide you to experience the state of shock as it is for you.

You might imagine a situation recently where you felt some fear or discomfort.

Perhaps you felt pressure or anger from someone, you felt rejected or ignored, or someone was disrespectful to you in some way.

Imagine that you are in that situation right now.

We invite you to begin to notice what happens in your body if you imagine this situation right now.

You may notice tightening in your throat and chest, shallow breathing, racing or confused thoughts, difficulty concentrating.

Let yourself gently tune in to this shock state and allow it to be there.

Touch it with your breath, bringing more awareness to however you experience it.

Perhaps there are other experiences in your body—headaches, backaches, cramps, disturbances in your digestion with diarrhea or constipation, or difficulty sleeping or feeling chronically tired.

If your fear is showing itself as agitation, rushing, shock, or body symptoms, we invite you to stay very attentive to these signs.

Allow yourself to slow down and tune in to these signs.

Breathe slowly and deeply as you feel them.

Imagine that you are being very attentive to a little child inside of you who is experiencing fear.

Feel her or him.

Perhaps picture her or him, knowing that this fear and shock has been there a long time. Only right now, it has been provoked and is showing itself.

Give yourself lots of time and lots of space to be with the fear and the frozenness, as if you are focusing all of your awareness and intensity on the fear in your body.

Be as present as you can to whatever you notice in your body or your mind.

If you feel overwhelmed, allow yourself to feel that too; this can be part of the shock.

Perhaps you notice that there are thoughts that tell you that you are weak or a failure.

There may be a voice saying, "I can't move. I can't do anything. I'm paralyzed. It's all too much! Pull yourself together! Stop being so afraid! Do something!"

If these thoughts are there, allow them to be there and watch them.

Bring warmth with your awareness as if you could melt the frozenness and soothe the anxiety with your love.

Imagine that your heart is sending out love and melting this frozenness.

Allow the vibrations of the heart to melt the shock.

When you find yourself in frightening situations and are in the grip of your fear or shock, allow yourself to slow down. Stay with yourself, moment to moment, and realize that you can slow down and breathe consciously.

It is very healing to take your time, to stay with yourself.

If fear or shock arises, let it be there without judging yourself. .

This love and understanding brings a deep acceptance.

Loving yourself, even when there's fear, reveals your deepest sensitivity and uncovers a hidden treasure.

CHAPTER 11:

FEAR THINKING

Not only is it important to observe the body symptoms that fear provokes, but it is also important to observe our fear minds. We have mentioned that healing fear involves seeing how we avoid feeling it, exploring its origin, noticing what triggers it today, and becoming aware of the body sensations associated with fear.

An additional important aspect of healing fear and shock is *becoming conscious of our fear thinking*.

Fear thinking consists of all the negative thoughts that come up when we have an experience of fear or shock.

It is common that when something triggers fear, negative thoughts arise very quickly. These thoughts include:

- "This is too much!"

- "I can't handle this."

- "Why is this happening to me?"

- "I have to get rid of this fear as quickly as possible!"

- "What can I do to make this go away?"

- "There is something terribly wrong with me that this is happening."

- "There is something wrong with the other person."

- "I have to defend myself."

- "It is impossible to trust anyone or life."

- "I must deserve this treatment."

- "I should be over this by now."

- "This shouldn't bother me; why does this bother me so much? "I am so weak and stupid."

When we are thinking these thoughts, it is difficult to stay present with the physical sensations in the body.

However, it is possible to watch our thoughts from some distance, understanding that they are coming from fear, and then gently begin to see the bigger perspective.

There are parallel positive thoughts that can support our exploration and our ability to stay present to fear and shock, such as:

- "I have the space inside to stay with this fear or shock."

- "If I stay with this experience and with these feelings, they will pass."

- "Learning to feel, observe, accept, and contain my fear is an essential step in my spiritual and emotional growth."

- "This experience of fear is happening as a challenge for me to gain more inner space."

- "It is only intense at first. After some time, my nervous system will slowly settle."

- "As I learn to stay with my fear and shock and even love this part of me, I am also gaining the ability to be intimate and go deep in love with another person."

- "I don't need and don't want to be rescued."

- "I don't need to do anything right now except feel and watch. It never leads to any good if I act from fear or if I distract myself from feeling."

- "If I need to take some action, I will wait until my nervous system settles and my inner wisdom arises."

It is a challenge not to get lost in the negative thoughts because they are an automatic result of our past traumas.

They are driven by fear; they are familiar, and very habitual.

Tanya is an intelligent, talented, energetic, and attractive forty-two-year-old woman. However, she is driven by compulsive fear thoughts that effectively sabotage her life. When she is with a man, she emphasizes the parts of him and of herself that she doesn't like, and she also imagines the worst happening in their relationship. She does the same with her work, perpetually finding the most difficult interpretations of every situation and problem she encounters. Her conversations are full of complaints.

Tanya assumes that anyone she comes close to or works with will betray or mistreat her, and then invariably, her prior assumptions become true. Her mistrustful fear thinking is so automatic that she does not even know that she is doing it. When we point it out to her, she says that it has been that way as long as she can remember, but she justifies her way of thinking by claiming that her experience proves her conclusions are correct. Of course, her childhood trauma from having a narcissistic mother who took all the space, an absent angry father, and parents who fought continually, helped conditioned her to look at life in a negative way. The problem with this kind of thinking is that the thoughts create reality. Part of Tanya's work now is to bring more awareness to her fear thinking and to recognize that the world and people are not necessarily as she assumes them to be. As she can consciously replaces these negative thoughts with positive ones, she will discover that her life will change.

Once we are taken over by these negative thoughts and believe them, we may easily sabotage our life energy, optimism, motivation to live a full and loving life, and the way others relate to us. Plus, we can easily feel overwhelmed because the thoughts propel us constantly into the red zone.

How can we switch to the bigger perspective and see the situation positively?

We teach three points of awareness to transform our negative, fear-driven thoughts.

1. *Become aware of our fear-driven thoughts,* noticing how automatic they are and how long they have operated in our lives.

2. Realize that when we have had experiences of actually passing through a panic episode, we come to know that *it will pass and we will get through it.*

3. Finally, the third point of awareness involves *actively replacing a negative, fear-driven thought with a positive one.*

Our thoughts will drive our lives. If we stop believing in the truth of our fear thoughts and replace them with a positive truth, it helps us to develop a new and different perspective on life.

We can practice this approach not only when we are experiencing fear, but also when we casually notice that we have taken a negative outlook on a situation in our lives.

These encouraging, loving thoughts are actually important truths that define the path toward emotional and spiritual growth.

They are essential stepping-stones, and they can help us in the moments of fear and despair.

Each one of these positive forms of thought that we have presented above is a different aspect of what we all can to learn to gain soul strength.

And rather than thoughts, they are more like an inner knowing or our wisdom guiding us.

Exercise:

We invite you to consider each one of the positive thoughts we have mentioned and take them deeply inside.

- See if you can feel them as true for your life.

- Consider how holding that thought might affect your life.

- The next time you experience fear:

  - See if you can notice the fear-driven thought that is behind the fear.

  - Practice consciously switching from the negative thought to this inner wisdom.

  - Feel how that movement might improve your ability to deal with the fear.

CHAPTER 12:

HOW WE REENACT OLD TRAUMAS

Maria is a thirty-two-year-old woman who has a history of entering into relationships with men who are violent and who abuse and humiliate her. In her own words, she has always been attracted to "bad boys." "They are exciting, the sex is hot, and I like the danger." She is attractive and sexy, dresses provocatively, freely admits that she uses drugs such as cocaine and marijuana at parties, and abuses alcohol. When she was a child her father had frequent outbursts of anger, and at those times would usually hit her mother. Both parents were often drunk. She retreated regularly to her room and created a fantasy world. As a teenager, she spent most of her time away from the house, used drugs, joined a wild crowd, and was sexually promiscuous. She comes to us because she recognizes that she cannot continue with the lifestyle she is living and would like to attract different kinds of men.

"If you look more deeply inside, what attracts you to a man who is violent and abusive?" we ask.

"The excitement makes me feel alive because inside I feel dead. Most of the time, especially when we are making love, I am not really there. But the violent sex is like a drug that helps me at least feel something."

"Have you always been with these kinds of men?"

"Well, a few times I was with softer ones who treated me better, but I could walk all over them. They couldn't handle my energy."

Maria is in deep shock and has a dramatic split between her traumatized and her functional selves.. She is attracted to violent men for many reasons, and these reasons propel her to act against her better judgment.

1. First of all, these men are much like her father. Her *original imprinting* of what a man is like is based on the kind of man her father was—selfish, violent, insensitive, and angry. We are naturally drawn to partners who in some basic ways resemble a parent. Unfortunately, that resemblance can be abusiveness. The imprint is that this is how our object of love should and will treat us.

2. Secondly, Maria's attraction to violence, wild sex, and drama *allows her to feel alive* because she feels dead inside. When we have deep shock, we may often seek power, drugs, wildness, extreme sports, violent sex, or intense conflict to feel anything at all.

3. Thirdly, she attracts a violent person because it takes this kind of energy to *penetrate her powerful defenses* and to make her feel vulnerable. She is not yet in a place where she would trust enough to voluntarily drop her armor, so she needs someone who can blast through. Unfortunately, this kind of dynamic only causes her to reenact her trauma, to feel less trust, and to go deeper into shock.

4. Finally, Maria is attracted to this kind of partner because she unconsciously believes that if she can learn *to stand up* to him, she will *master the trauma* she received from her father. If she can learn to confront her partner's violence in a way she never could with her

father, she will be able to feel some sense of control and power in her life. A less powerful man would never do. In fact, if she were with a man who showed his vulnerability, she would become the abuser, judging and criticizing him.

Abuser, Abused, or Rescuer?

As a result of trauma, we may become the abuser, the abused, or the rescuer. When we have experienced violence or neglect as a child, we may go to one or other of the poles between abuser and abused.

Or we may also become a rescuer.

The rescuer is a common role if we had parents who abused substances or were emotionally unstable or unfulfilled in their lives. Rescuers believe that their mission and purpose in life is to save and help the person they are close to.

This is the case with Anna, a forty-five-year-old woman who is married to a man who regularly comes home drunk and then spends the evening watching football on television. This is the third time she has been with a man who abuses substances. The previous one was also an alcoholic, and the one before him was a drug addict. She was able to extract herself finally from those relationships when she realized that there was no hope that either would ever get clean. With her current husband, things started out well; the drinking only began to surface later. They have two children, ages eight and ten, so Anna is much less inclined to leave. She has asked her husband to stop drinking, and he makes promises that he then doesn't fulfill. Once, when she became very angry with him for drinking, he started a Twelve Step program, went to meetings, and even got a sponsor, but he quit after two months and never went back. Anna lives in the hope that with her love, she can get him to stop one day. It never worked with her father and it is not likely to work with her husband either.

The neglect from a parent or parents who abuse a substance is extreme because they are choosing to deal with their pain and anxiety in this dysfunctional way, their behavior is unpredictable, and they are never truly present for their child.

But neglect also happens in other ways, and when we have experienced neglect as a child, we are likely to reenact more neglect in our lives today.

Monica is a thirty-nine-year-old woman who works as a nurse at a general practice clinic. She is attractive, loving, sensitive, and deep, but her relationships with men have been unfortunate. She is the youngest of four siblings and frequently felt ignored as a child. She knows that her mother's pregnancy with her was a mistake and she doubts if her mother really wanted another child. Indirectly, she felt that she came as an unwanted additional responsibility. Her father was absent from the home and took no part in the raising of the children. Her mother was preoccupied with an older sister who had learning disabilities. Monica became accustomed to being alone and to feeling unwanted by both her parents. As an adult, she found herself attracted to men who were unavailable for one reason or another. Her greatest heartbreak was when she became involved with a doctor at her clinic. She had a passionate affair with him, but he could not leave his wife, and in the end left her.

When we have become used to rejection, our nervous systems anticipates it.

Rather than feel the pain of yet another rejection, we may find someone who is unlikely to ever be truly available.

To our unconscious traumatized minds, this kind of preprogrammed rejection seems easier to deal with than what could happen if we lost control and surrendered ourselves to a love that had no forgone conclusion.

So we go for what is known.

We reenact trauma not only in our relationships but also in our creative expression. This pattern can cause us to stifle and sabotage our creativity and our lives energy.

As a child, we naturally needed support and guidance to discover and express our gifts and our natural, unique passions and talents.

This process became suppressed if we lacked this support, or worse, if we experienced humiliation, criticism, unreasonable pressure, and expectations, or pressure to become someone and do something that we were not meant to be or do.

Sometimes a parent or teacher feels threatened or jealous when a child is different, successful, or very alive. The child's uniqueness may threaten the rules that they live by and keep them secure. When we were a child, our energy may have made parents or teachers question their own life choices. Rather than deal with their fears, they may have humiliated and repressed us. The same can be true for teachers and the whole environment we have been raised in.

Often one or both parent's expectations result in the child having to compete and be pressured to be the best. This pressure may cause tremendous disturbance inside or a feeling that we can never do enough to earn the respect we long for. Today when we attempt to express ourselves, we may feel all that pressure again. So we may endlessly push ourselves or unconsciously choose to give up. It may never have been in our nature to compete, and this giving up can also be an unconscious way of rebelling against our parents.

Alison is a twenty-one-year-old woman who is referred to us for counseling because she is experiencing chronic low energy, lack of motivation, and unexplainable pains in her body. When she arrives for the session, she sits passively and answers the questions in a disconnected and seemingly unconcerned way. She was raised in a strictly religious family with a great deal of pressure to succeed, "be a nice girl," and always do well at whatever she undertakes. Furthermore, she always felt inferior to her older sister, who was more aggressive, social, and outgoing than she was and still is. Alicia's depression is really a passive resistance to all the pressure and expectations she received. By nature, she is a deeply sensitive and introverted person whose way is totally opposite to that of her parents and sister. Through regular sessions, she begins to understand that she is different than the rest of the family and that her low energy is a dysfunctional way of saying "no!" She starts to discover new ways to find and be herself.

Unless we have tremendous strength to persevere against this kind of negative energy, our motivation to discover ourselves will not happen as it should.

We may be too afraid to provoke the anger or rejection of "the big people."

Instead we may lack motivation or sabotage any efforts to express ourselves.

It is as if there is a hidden force inside us stopping our expansion. That hidden force comes from the influences from our past that put us down when we were vulnerable and impressionable and were not tuned in to who we were as a person.

There is also another significant way that we reenact trauma, and it occurs because as children, we all are highly impressionable and curious.

We have a hunger to learn, and unfortunately, much of this learning could come from parents who did not have good skills to deal with life.

One of our most important lessons is how to deal with fear and pain.

If we witnessed our parents feeling, accepting, and showing their vulnerability in a healthy way, we learned to do the same.

But if we watched them dealing with their pain and fear by abusing alcohol or drugs, by overeating or starving themselves, by becoming depressed, or by raging, then that is what we learned.

Antonio's father was both an alcoholic and a rage-aholic. He came home drunk on a regular basis, and whenever he became stressed with finances or something was not to his liking at home, he would yell and blame someone. His grandfather was the same way. Because Antonio is aware of his family history, he has been careful not to drink, but he has not been able to avoid the other addiction from his past. He rages at his wife whenever he is upset.

The imprinting of this kind of trauma is very deep. If we experience pain or fear in your lives today, there is a strong unconscious pull to take the same path one or both of our parents took.

Putting a Stop to Repetitive Patterns

Clearly, when we discuss repetitive patterns, the question arises: *How can we put a stop to them?*

1. The first step toward ending these patterns is to recognize them and see the connection to our earlier life experience. This begins the process of recovery.

2. Then it is important to feel the pain of the pattern and to reach a point in our lives when the pain of continuing is worse than the fear and pain connected to dropping it.

3. Finally, once we have recognized the pattern and explored it deeply, we can discover that *our previous choices were made from a space of shame and fear.* Now, we can realize whether we are acting from fear or making *better choices that are motivated from appreciating ourselves.*

Exercise:

Taking a look at your life, see if you can identify a familiar pattern.

- Do you tend to re-create rejection by being with people who are unavailable?

- Do you tend to be attracted to partners or friends who are violent, unkind, or even humiliating?

- Do you have a tendency to drink, overeat, get angry, or sink into depression when you feel stressed or overwhelmed?

- Do you get irritated or angry when things are not the way you would like?

- If you notice any of these tendencies, did one or both of those who raised you do the same?

- What is the price you pay for living in this pattern?

- Can you recognize if you are acting from fear and/or shame?

- How would it feel if you acted from a space of loving and appreciating yourself?

- Would you choose differently, and what would you risk and fear if you made different choices?

CHAPTER 13:

FINDING OUR PROTECTOR

Myriam, a sensitive, intelligent, and beautiful woman aged fifty-one, had a terribly traumatic childhood. She was sexually abused by her father from ages six to ten, and her mother was consistently mean, critical, and unloving with her. Fortunately, she found the fortitude to escape from her home when she was sixteen and found ways to survive on her own by finding work and a place to live. In her relationships with men, she used her attractiveness and sexuality to feel worthy of their affections but never felt nourished or happy. Eventually, she married a very wealthy man, who gave her financial security but abused her sexually and emotionally. She was so shocked that she did not even realize she was being mistreated by him, let alone set a limit. When she finally realized how unhappy she felt in her marriage, she got a divorce. Two years ago, she began intensive therapy with us, and much has changed. Her greatest achievement has been that now she is aware and can set limits when she feels disrespected. She continues to have a nonsexual connection with her ex-husband, but now she is able to be very clear and straight with him. This has been a huge growth for her.

We move now into the last aspect of dealing and working with our fears. Up to now, our approach has focused on understanding more about fear, how it feels, where it comes from, what triggers it, and learning to be present to our fear and shock as it arises in our everyday lives. In the next few chapters, we work on a more active aspect. This has to do with risk and learning to stand up for ourselves, as Myriam did.

As children, we didn't have the resources to deal with not being given the security and protection we needed.

We didn't have the strength to deal with an invasion or disrespect to our young developing boundaries.

As children, we couldn't even imagine why someone would want to violate us or not care for us, because in our innocent and trusting state, we only understand love.

And because we so desperately needed love and approval, we gave up our self-respect and our boundaries.

As children, we were unable to express our hurt when we were neglected, or to say no when we were being repressed, given unreasonable rules or expectations, conditioned to assume roles that were not appropriate for our ages, or humiliated with criticism or judgments.

We couldn't say "stop!" when a parent was raging, beating us, or invading us.

And even today, we may find it hard or impossible to feel when we are being disrespected.

We are unable to set limits because we may have become so used to being invaded.

We may not have connection to our natural sense of personal boundaries and to the place deep inside that knows when something is not right.

When we were traumatized and abused as children, we lost touch with this basic sense.

We stopped listening to it and became accustomed to humiliation and abuse.

Today, when similar invasions happen, we may not realize that we are being disrespected.

It may not even occur to us to stand up for ourselves and to say something, or walk away.

Or if it does occur to us that something is not right, we may be too afraid to say or do anything—too afraid of the other person's anger, rejection, punishment, or further abuse.

A big part of our healing process is to retrieve the sense of our boundaries, to feel that we have a right to be respected in those boundaries, and to feel the basic sense of "this is not right" when someone is disrespectful to our boundaries.

We need to create the protector that we lacked as children.

The protector is an empowered energy that stands in front of our vulnerable selves, our traumatized, shocked and frightened child, and defends us against insults, humiliation, abuse, and any kind of disrespect.

In order to find our protector, we must be able *to feel the anger of being invaded and disrespected.*

In addition to fear, some other things stand in the way of creating our protector:

1. We may have the conditioning that we have *to be polite.*

2. We may have a tendency to *minimize or deny* a hurt when we receive it.

3. We may *excuse, forgive, or analyze* the person who is invading us instead of feeling the impact and results of being invaded.

4. We may feel more comfortable with the emotion of sadness rather than anger. Perhaps it wasn't safe to get angry as a child because perhaps we may have been judged, abused, or punished for being angry.

5. We may be so accustomed to being disrespected that *it does not feel insulting* anymore; it feels *normal.*

6. Deep inside, we don't believe *we are worthy of respect.*

Finding the protector inside begins with understanding what it means to have our boundaries invaded.

Every person has the birthright to have his or her physical, sexual, emotional, and spiritual boundaries respected.

This means not being told what to believe, what to do, what to think, how to feel, what to dream and not to dream for, and how to live our lives.

We all need honesty, consistency, reliability, and accountability from the people we are close to. And if we don't receive this, we might move to one of the dysfunctional ways of being, such as becoming chronically angry or depressed, pulling away, or going to an addiction.

A healthier, more functional way of living is to honor our personal space, feel when we are being disrespected, to express our feelings, and to set a limit if that is needed in the situation.

Here are some examples of direct invasions:

- When someone *tells us what we are thinking or feeling and what we should do or say* without our having asked for advice.

- When someone *makes an appointment and consistently comes late or not at all.*

- When someone *threatens us* in any way—with *violence, rejection, punishment, or silence.*

- When we experience *violence, judgments, demands, pressure, expectations, or criticism* from someone.

- When someone is *disrespectful to our possessions, or borrows money and doesn't pay it back.*

- When someone *doesn't respect our "no!"*

- When we are continually *interrupted* and if the other person takes all the space.

All of these are invasions of our boundaries.

When our boundaries are invaded, we need to learn to bring in our protector to say "no!" or "stop," or "this is not okay for me!"

In the next chapters, we will describe how to find and create your protector.

Exercise:

Take a moment to consider why it is hard for you to say no, to set a limit, or to get angry.

- Do you have an idea that you have to be polite and avoid conflict at all costs?

- Are you afraid of provoking the anger or punishment of the other person?

- Are you afraid that you might be rejected if you stand up for yourself?

- Are you quick to excuse and "understand" the other person?

- Was anger too dangerous a feeling to feel when you were young?

- Did you get used to being mistreated and come to accept it?

- Do you feel that deep inside you are not worthy of being treated with respect?

CHAPTER 14:

THE THREE STAGES OF EMPOWERMENT

I magine that you are in a supermarket and you happen to notice a scene between a mother and a child. The mother is angry because the little girl continues to take toys off the shelves and put them into the grocery cart. The mother puts the toys back on the shelf and yells at the child to behave herself. But the child is stubborn and persistent and keeps taking the toys and throwing them into the trolley. Finally, the mother begins to shake the child very hard, yelling at her to stop and behave herself. When the little girl begins to cry, the mother smacks her in the face and tells her to be quiet. The girl cries even louder and the mother hits her again.

- Imagine that you are this little girl. What would you feel? What would happen to you inside? What might be the effect on you from being treated in this way?

- As the bystander, what kind of emotion do you feel after watching this scene?

- And if you were to intervene between the mother and the child, what do you imagine you might say to the mother?

We tell you this story because it helps to outline what we call "the three stages of empowerment."

Probably this child will experience lasting fear, shock, and shame from being treated in this way.

Perhaps you might feel some anger at the mother for abusing the child in this way.

Or you might feel the helplessness and desperation of the mother and understand her feelings.

Perhaps if you were to intervene, you might say to the mother:

"Stop. You are hurting her. There is another way to deal with this situation instead of using violence! I understand that you are desperate, but let's see if we can find another way."

You would be temporarily taking on the role of protector for this child. But as long as the mother continued to treat her this way, the girl would be at risk of experiencing a childhood filled with fear and shock, and would be powerless to change the negative direction of her life.

In our experience, the ability to feel and live our power – find our ability to set limits clearly and nonviolently, we find that we will go through three states. They are seldom linear, but each stage is an aspect of process.

1. *Awareness of shame, shock, and fear and identifying the negative belief*

2. *Feeling the anger of invasion*

3. *Setting limits with clarity and heart.*

Stage 1: Awareness of Shame, Shock, and Fear and Identifying the Negative Belief

In the first stage, we are *becoming aware of when and how we get and got invaded and the effect that these invasions have upon us.*

It is already a huge step when we are no longer living in denial or being oblivious to incidents when we are being disrespected.

At this stage, we cannot respond or even feel angry.

But we may begin to *feel the fear, shock, and shame that are there.*

Also, when we are in this state, it can help to *identify a shame-driven or fear-driven belief* that holds us in the shame, fear, or shock.

This is all part of the first stage of empowerment.

It is profoundly empowering simply to become aware of how deep and how frequent our fear and shock are, how easily these feelings may get triggered, and how we experience them.

Stage 2: Feeling the Anger of Invasion

But there comes a time as we allow ourselves to feel shock, fear, and the shame of being disrespected when we start to feel some anger arising.

We begin to sense that it was and is not right to be treated this way.

When we bring more dignity to ourselves, we naturally begin to feel outrage at someone invading our lives with his or her opinions, judgments, criticism, threats, pressure, expectations, and aggression.

And when this healthy anger begins to surface, we are entering into the second stage of empowerment.

This is a big step, because as we discussed in the last chapter, it might be difficult for us to allow ourselves to feel anger.

But anger is the healthy and natural emotion to feel when our boundaries are not respected.

It was the emotion that perhaps we could not feel as a child, but now we are strong and big enough to allow it to arise from inside of us.

The anger of the second stage of empowerment is not the anger we feel when we are irritated that things are not going the way we want, or the anger we feel when we get impatient or overwhelmed, or the anger of feeling frustrated when we are not getting what we want from someone or from life.

It is the anger that re-affirms our sense of self.

It is like a deep fire inside that begins to wake up—a fire of dignity and self-respect.

Our true life energy wants to expand and to live.

When we begin to get in touch with this fire inside, it will very likely produce intense fear and guilt because:

1. We might have been threatened, shamed, punished, beaten, or rejected in the past when we expressed energy or rebellion.

2. We repressed this life energy very early because we were taught that it is not polite to be angry or create a disturbance.

3. It is too frightening to step away from the crowd, from our family, and our environment and become our own person.

And as a result we may have learned to shrink our energy and become small.

We may have a lot of built-up resentments inside for being so profoundly repressed in our vital life energy.

Patrick was intimidated from an early age by his father's anger and beatings and his mother's controlling behavior. When he first came to work with us, he was extremely timid and soft-spoken. He continued to have a close connection to both his parents, even though they continued to abuse him. He was not able to understand the effect this treatment had on him. However, as the work progressed, Patrick slowly began to connect with some anger. At first, it caused him to feel so guilty and frightened that he quickly suppressed it, but soon he began to enjoy the feeling of his anger and the sense of power it gave him. We suggested he work with it in a healthy way by taking boxing classes, and he loved them.

The second stage of empowerment is awakening and making friends with this anger.

Anger is in essence an energy of protection and assertion of dignity.

Naturally, we may fear that when we do get in touch with the anger inside us we could hurt someone or ourselves and lose control.

Therefore, the best way to work with the rage of the second stage is to do it in environments that are safe, such as doing kickboxing in a gym, working individually with a therapist, or doing workshops where we can safely express this energy without hurting ourselves or someone else.

In this stage of empowerment, our anger is generally not limited to the situation that has provoked us. It also contains all the anger we have built up from prior invasions in our lives where we could not express or defend ourselves.

In our work, we don't encourage people to take out their anger on their partner, friend, parent, or child because when we are raging at someone, it is not truly empowering, and furthermore, it can deeply damage the trust between us and the other person.

It will probably happen when we are close to someone, that we have an outburst of anger. That's fine as long as we use that energy to go deeper with ourselves and with the other person. It can be a stepping-stone to more honest communication.

It is not okay if it's simply an unconscious venting.

Stage 3: Setting Limits with Clarity

True and lasting empowerment comes at the third stage.

Here, we learn to stand up for ourselves and for our energy and our needs, and, if necessary, to set clear, appropriate, and assertive limits.

In the third stage of empowerment, we are no longer blinded by an emotional space.

Our power lies in our clarity and in our confidence in being able to feel ourselves and to protect our boundaries.

Self-respect develops as we are able to feel what is right for us and to set clear limits to specific behaviors.

When we set a limit in the third stage, we are not saying "no" to the other person, but rather setting a limit to a certain behavior. Naturally, it takes time to find the clarity and courage to do this in real life.

But we can practice with a friend or a therapist, as Andrea's story illustrates:

Andrea, a forty-six-year-old woman, is currently in a difficult relationship with a Peter. Peter has been wounded himself, so he protects himself by being very concerned about his own needs and doesn't easily recognize her or her needs. She admires his energy, fortitude, perseverance, and confidence but gets infuriated with his selfishness. She has been with him for nine years, and during this time—thanks to her commitment to ongoing individual therapy and seminars—she has progressed through the three stages of empowerment. At first, Peter's dominating behavior only brought up her shame and shock. She was feeling very insecure and constantly judged and doubted herself. She could not feel her own needs or when he was invasive and disrespectful. It never occurred to her that she needed mutual vulnerability and respect. But gradually, she began to feel the rage inside that was also connected to her mother's equally selfish ways. To help her anger awaken, she joined a kickboxing class at her local gym.

Andrea started raging at Peter but these outbreaks of anger only made their connection worse. She recognized that it was good for her to feel the anger, but this way of reacting and fighting with him was not helping. As she began to love herself, she could also validate her needs for recognition and respect and realized that she could no longer bend her life around him and give up her creativity and her friends. At first, she practiced how to set clear limits with him with her therapist. She had to work through all her fears that he would not listen or understand, that he would rage back at her, or that he would leave her. But at this point, she knew that she would rather have her dignity than continue giving up herself and getting bitter, angry, and resentful. Eventually, Andrea found the courage to speak to him directly and express her needs. This clarity from her side woke him up, and he realized that if he wanted to keep this relationship, he too needed to take a good look at himself. He began ongoing therapy.

Exercise:

Take a moment to consider the significant relationships in your life.

Is there anyone with whom you feel disrespected or invaded?

If so, what is the way he or she is disrespecting you?

- Telling you what you should do, think, or say?

- Consistently coming late or not coming to an appointment?

- Threatening you in some way with aggression, rejection, or withholding attention or money?

- Being aggressive with you through actions or words?

- Not respecting you when you set a limit?

What do you feel inside when you receive this kind of treatment?

- Do you go into fear or shock?

- Do you feel shame?

- Do you feel anger?

Imagine saying something to this person such as:

- "It is not okay for me when you ... !"

- "It is hard for me to be open to you when you ..."

Then allow yourself to feel whatever fear or guilt comes up when you imagine saying this.

CHAPTER 15:

BUILDING A CONTAINER

W hen we are in fear, it is easy to feel overwhelmed. We are probably frantic that we must do something immediately to change the situation, and it can seem like a matter of life and death when fear takes over.

To deal with fear, we need to build a container.

The container is the foundation for going through all the aspects of working with fear that we have described. It gives us the ability to be present to fear, to allow it to move through us and pass away.

When building a container, it might help to imagine that your belly is a soft, loving, and embracing womb that can hold the part of you that experiences fear—your frightened/shocked child.

Normally, when we have fear, we feel that this is all we are. We don't have the experience or the awareness that this feeling is only a part of us that takes over when our trauma is provoked.

To build a container, we have to introduce you to the understanding that all of us have two states of consciousness living side by side inside of us.

One state is that of *the wounded, traumatized, frightened child.*

This part of us lives in fear, and its thinking, behavior, and inner experience is driven by fear.

The other is *the mature adult state of consciousness.*

This part of us has the ability to detach itself from the fear experience and to become aware of when, how, and why fear arises, how it feels in the body, how it thinks, and how it drives our behaviors.

The mature adult state of consciousness becomes like a mother or father to our frightened child.

Doris is a highly attractive and intelligent forty-year-old woman who suffers from frequent panic attacks that began only recently. Her father is a wealthy businessman, and she was raised in high-class society, accustomed to luxury and servants. Her mother was depressed and violent and committed suicide when Doris was twelve. Her father had frequent temper tantrums, and Doris assumed the role of her father's confidant and tried to soothe him when he was upset. Some years ago, he suffered serious financial problems that involved court cases for tax evasion and eventual bankruptcy. Doris married a loving but emotionally disconnected man who took care of her financially, but the relationship ended when she had an affair.

Doris had never created a container. She had been pampered as a child and continued to live in her child state of consciousness as an adult, emotionally tied to her irresponsible father and married to a man who took care of her. When her lifeboat sank with the financial crisis of her father and the breakup of the marriage, her frightened child took over, causing her frequent panic attacks. Her healing task has been to strengthen her resources and create a container to hold the fears of her child caused by her childhood traumas.

Imagine that a container is like a strong embracing and holding energy that is capable of reassuring the emotional, frightened part of you that everything is going to be all right.

Imagine that this energy is like a mature motherly or fatherly energy holding and reassuring the frightened child.

Once we have some awareness of this container—the adult embracing part of us—we can consciously switch our awareness from the disturbance inside to the container. We can switch our awareness from the agitated, activated child part to the calm, centered adult part of us.

Imagine that this reassuring, centered energy is soothing the fear and anxiety.

It has strong arms and body to hold the fears, embracing the fears with confidence and presence.

To build these strong arms and body, it helps to actually strengthen the skeletal muscles of our body—the muscles of the arms, legs, and trunk.

Any kind of muscle-training exercises can be of immense support toward building more strength in our skeletal musculature—fitness training, Pilates, or yoga, for example.

As these muscles become stronger, we can more easily begin to feel and identify with the mature adult part of us.

Then, when fear arises, we can imagine that our awareness is switching to our mature adult, holding our anxious child.

Exercise:

A Guided Meditation on Building a Container

(You can record this meditation and play it back to yourself, or you can have a friend read it to you.)

Take a moment to sit in a quiet place where you can be undisturbed for the length of this meditation.

Recall a recent time when something or someone disturbed you.

Take a few moments to remember this incident and what it was specifically that bothered you.

Allow yourself gently to feel this disturbance.

Notice the anxiety, irritation, or anger that may have been provoked in you.

Notice how these feel in your body.

You may notice how you energetically try to protect yourself, either by closing or by pushing the other person away.

Observe the thoughts that come with this incident, if there are thoughts—thoughts about yourself, about the other person, or about the situation.

Notice how you might have behaved in this situation—just observing.

Now imagine that all these feelings and thoughts and behavior are coming from a young wounded part of you that feels threatened and unsafe.

This part of you has been activated.

Just breathe into it—feeling it—and letting it be there.

As you continue to use your breath to soothe the anxiety, something may begin to settle.

Now slowly begin to switch your awareness to the mature adult part of you that has strength and calmness.

Imagine that this adult part is holding the frightened, agitated part in the belly, and you are surrounding her or him with love and security.

You are gently holding and embracing this young wounded part of you...

Holding her or him with your love and presence and compassion...

No need to do anything, just holding and embracing her or him...

Feeling that your breath and your presence are soothing and comforting this child...

You are noticing perhaps that there is now more relaxation even in this fragile, wounded part of you.

CHAPTER 16:

BUILDING OUR STRENGTH AND RESOURCES

C oming out of fear and shock is a slow process.
Our nervous systems have been deeply traumatized, and it takes time to recover the strength and dignity that we have lost.

Our nervous systems have been conditioned to survive and defend us from impossibly frightening situations by spacing out and freezing.

Now we are learning to come back to the natural ways our nervous systems respond to a threat—either through fight or flight—by either confronting or going away from the threat.

As we heal, we begin to find the courage and the ability to do that by empowering our bodies and minds.

When we have been traumatized, it is natural to fold in on our energy and become less alive.

It is natural to sink into a lower level of life energy because aliveness could invite further trauma.

Also, when we are traumatized, it is easy to adopt a negative attitude toward life, others, and ourselves.

Persistent negative attitudes and thoughts have a seriously detrimental effect on our states of mind, life, and health.

It is important to take some active steps in the opposite direction—toward a vital feeling in the body and a positive attitude in the mind.

Here are ten suggestions that can help you build resources:

1. Make a habit of *moving your body* on a regular basis.

2. Practice *assertion of your energy* and anger in a safe and protected environment.

3. Find a *coach, trainer, and/or therapist* to help you with the above; particularly in the beginning to help get your energy moving.

4. Find and cultivate *hobbies* that give you *joy and inspiration*.

5. Surround yourself with *people who support* your growth and empowerment.

6. Spend as *little time as possible or none at all* with family members or friends who continue to repeat old *disrespectful behavior toward you* or who live in negativity. Alternately, if you are with them, be as aware as possible what is happening to you.

7. Look at your relationships with the people close to you to see if you need *to make amends* for some ways that you may have been unkind or disrespectful toward them.

8. When you feel ready, see if you can directly *set a limit* with someone whom you feel has disrespected you in the ways we have described. This may be necessary if you have cut off from the person because you did not speak out about something that was hurtful.

9. Become aware of the *negative statements you carry inside* about yourself, others, and life, and know that these are the result of trauma.

10. As often and as consistently as possible, question your automatic negative thoughts, look at them, and feel them from your heart and your wisdom. See how your heart would *rephrase these statements* so they become life affirmative and encouraging.

11. You can find a way *to sooth your nervous system* by spending quiet time with yourself perhaps sitting in meditation, taking walks or runs in nature, listening to soothing music, or enjoying a relaxing bath.

CONCLUSION:

I n this handbook, we have attempted to present a concise and practical approach toward healing shame, insecurity, fear, and shock.

In this process of healing, our challenge is to rediscover the original trust and innocence that we had as a child.

Except now, as an adult, we can re-attain these wonderful qualities, with the maturity that can accept and embrace the fears and insecurity we have inside and recognize that life is a journey of learning to come alive in spite of these wounds.

We may be able to understand and accept that life brings both pain and joy; agony and ecstasy. And unless we take the inner journey to discover our true being that never changes, we will always be suffering.

If we do not take the inner journey, it is highly likely that we will live a life of suffering, boredom, mistrust, and isolation.

We may chronically blame or complain.

And we may use the painful experiences that life brings us to deepen our mistrust rather than use them as opportunities to grow.

For instance:

- We have opened to someone, and we discover that he or she is not as loving or as present with us as we had hoped.

- We have experienced a painful rejection or loss.

- A friend has spoken badly about us behind our back.

- We have discovered that our lover is having an affair.

- We feel misunderstood by someone close to us.

- Someone has been dishonest with us.

- We have been fired at work or didn't get the job we would have liked.

- We have been unjustly accused or judged.

- We have been excluded by someone or by a group.

Before we undertake the journey of healing, it is easy for us to believe and feel that the world is against us when we encounter these kinds of difficult and painful situations.

Or to feel that no matter how hard we try, things don't seem to get better.

It is easy to become bitter or angry or to go into resignation and depression.

The journey of healing teaches us that current events in our lives are a repeat of earlier wounds.

They are challenges that life brings us as an opportunity to heal by feeling the pain of what we went through and by taking positive steps in the direction of self-actualizing.

When we take a journey of healing and we change our perspectives and attitudes, our whole approach toward life changes.

We may discover that we no longer live in blame and negativity.

Something becomes softer inside, and we may no longer be fighting with life and with what it brings.

Gratitude arises, and we can begin to see and love ourselves in a new way.

We begin to feel the tremendous honor and respect of being given this life as an opportunity to grow.

Recognizing and learning to accept our shame, insecurities, shock, and fear makes us human.

It softens our edges and helps us to appreciate the beauty of life, even with the pain and difficulties.

With much love and support for your ongoing journey,

Krishnananda and Amana

SELECTED REFERENCES

Bradshaw, John. _Healing the Shame That Binds You._ Deerfield Park, FL: Health Communications, 1988.

Brown, Byron. _Soul without Shame._ Boston: Shambala, 1999.

Kaufman, Gresham. _The Psychology of Shame._ New York: Springer Publishing, 1996.

Krishnananda Trobe, and Amana Trobe. _Face to Face with Fear: Transforming Fear into Love._ Cambridge: Perfect Publisher LMD, 2005.

Krishnananda Trobe, and Amana Trobe. _From Fantasy Trust to Real Trust: Learning from Our Disappointments and Betrayals._ Sedona, AZ: Learning Love Publications, 2011.

Krishnananda Trobe, and Amana Trobe. _The Learning Love Handbook, Book 1: Opening to Vulnerability._ Sedona, AZ: Learning Love Publications, 2013.

Krishnananda Trobe, and Amana Trobe. *Stepping Out of Fear: Breaking Free of Our Pain and Suffering.* Sedona, AZ: Learning Love Publications, 2013.

Krishnananda Trobe, and Amana Trobe. *When Sex Becomes Vulnerable: How Our Sexuality Changes as the Relationship Deepens.* Strategic Publishing, 2008.

Levine, Peter. *In an Unspoken Voice.* Berkeley, CA: North Atlantic Books, 2010.

Levine, Peter. *Waking the Tiger.* Berkeley, CA: North Atlantic Books, 1997.

Rothschild, Babette. *The Body Remembers.* New York: W.W. Norton, 2000.

Made in the USA
Charleston, SC
25 April 2014